It was only a matter of time before a clever publisher realized that there is an audience for whom *Exile on Main Street* or *Electric Ladyland* are as significant and worthy of study as *The Catcher in the Rye* or *Middlemarch* … The series … is freewheeling and eclectic, ranging from minute rock-geek analysis to idiosyncratic personal celebration — *The New York Times Book Review*

Ideal for the rock geek who thinks liner notes just aren't enough — *Rolling Stone*

One of the coolest publishing imprints on the planet — *Bookslut*

These are for the insane collectors out there who appreciate fantastic design, well-executed thinking, and things that make your house look cool. Each volume in this series takes a seminal album and breaks it down in startling minutiae. We love these. We are huge nerds — *Vice*

A brilliant series … each one a work of real love — *NME* (UK)

Passionate, obsessive, and smart — *Nylon*

Religious tracts for the rock 'n' roll faithful — *Boldtype*

[A] consistently excellent series — *Uncut* (UK)

We … aren't naive enough to think that we're your only source for reading about music (but if we had our way … watch out). For those of you who really like to know everything there is to know about an album, you'd do well to check out Bloomsbury's "33 1/3" series of books — *Pitchfork*

For almost 20 years, the 33-and-a-Third series of music books has focused on individual albums by acts well known (Bob Dylan, Nirvana, Abba, Radiohead), cultish (Neutral Milk Hotel, Throbbing Gristle, Wire) and many levels in-between. The range of music and their creators defines "eclectic," while the writing veers from freewheeling to acutely insightful. In essence, the books are for the music fan who (as Rolling Stone noted) "thinks liner notes just aren't enough." — *The Irish Times*

For reviews of individual titles in the series, please visit our blog at 333sound.com and our website at https://www.bloomsbury.com/academic/music-sound-studies/

Follow us on Twitter: @333books

Like us on Facebook: https://www.facebook.com/33.3books

For a complete list of books in this series, see the back of this book.

Forthcoming in the series:

Shout at the Devil by Micco Caporale
White Limozeen by Steacy Easton
I'm Wide Awake, It's Morning by Holden Seidlitz
Hounds of Love by Leah Kardos
Re by Carmelo Esterrich
New Amerykah Part Two (Return of the Ankh)
by Kameryn Alexa Carter
In the Life of Chris Gaines by Stephen Deusner
and many more …

101

Mary Valle

BLOOMSBURY ACADEMIC
NEW YORK · LONDON · OXFORD · NEW DELHI · SYDNEY

BLOOMSBURY ACADEMIC
Bloomsbury Publishing Inc
1385 Broadway, New York, NY 10018, USA
50 Bedford Square, London, WC1B 3DP, UK
29 Earlsfort Terrace, Dublin 2, Ireland

BLOOMSBURY, BLOOMSBURY ACADEMIC and the
Diana logo are trademarks of Bloomsbury Publishing Plc

First published in the United States of America 2024

Bloomsbury Publishing Inc does not have any control over, or responsibility
for, any third-party websites referred to or in this book. All internet
addresses given in this book were correct at the time of going to
press. The author and publisher regret any inconvenience caused if
addresses have changed or sites have ceased to exist, but can
accept no responsibility for any such changes.

Whilst every effort has been made to locate copyright holders the publishers
would be grateful to hear from any person(s) not here acknowledged.

A catalog record for this book is available from the Library of Congress.

ISBN: PB: 978-1-5013-9032-6
         ePDF: 978-1-5013-9034-0
         eBook: 978-1-5013-9033-3

Series: 33 1/3

Typeset by Integra Software Services Pvt. Ltd.
Printed and bound in Great Britain

To find out more about our authors and books visit www.bloomsbury.com
and sign up for our newsletters.

For Josh and Margaret

Contents

Introduction

"We have Depeche Mode, and I'm just going to describe that they are all wearing black leather,"[1] says Richard Blade, broadcasting live on KROQ from the Rose Bowl in Pasadena, California.

Blade, an expatriate Brit and popular DJ at the influential "alternative" FM station, is DM's No. 1 stateside fan and booster.

It's a cool April morning in 1988. DM—an English electronic band composed of singer Dave Gahan, songwriter Martin Gore, sound wizard and classically trained musician Alan Wilder, and utility player, the late Andy "Fletch" Fletcher (who recently died at the time of writing this book), clad in black leather biker jackets, are riding onto the Rose Bowl's field in a vintage Cadillac. Like many rock band-related affairs, it's a bit ludicrous and "Spinal Tap"-esque. The open-air Caddy gives them the air of a touring cast of "Grease" in a small-town Fourth of July parade, but there aren't any townsfolk on hand to wave to the singing greasers. Touchingly, Blade is beaming with pride in the accomplishments of his "boys from Basildon."

The boys are here to announce their upcoming KROQ-hosted "A Concert for the Masses," the 101st and final concert of their world tour supporting *Music for the Masses*, DM's sixth studio album. It's a significant risk: the band lacks traditional markers of popularity such as high album sales, hit singles, and critical acclaim, and has topped out American concert attendance at around 20,000. DM's avid SoCal fan base, fueled by KROQ's dedicated support, turns out in droves. 65,000 souls reported for duty, filling the stadium.

Alan Wilder the group's musical wizard, steps up to a microphone. He's sheepish, awkward. His hair is perfectly sculpted.

The other lads are goofing off behind him. They always make Wilder do the things they are embarrassed to do. There's some fidgety business with his leather jacket. He's taken it off and is clutching it awkwardly to his chest.

Wilder is usually the literal coolest of the cool—"too cool for Depeche Mode," joked Gahan on the *101* film commentary—and has the supernatural ability to wear a leather jacket on a roasting summer night, under stadium-strength lighting, and remain cucumber-crispy, perfectly coiffed, all "I got this, clowns," attitude in spades.

Wilder announces that they will have a very special concert, the last of the tour, at the prestigious Rose Bowl and that there will be other bands as well.

The Modes are interviewed by various media outlets. Gore says, "Ni hao China, this is Martin Gore from Depeche Mode. I hope you like listening to our music." Fletcher, the group's tall, bespectacled, multipurpose utility man, goes long to catch a football and misses.

Two and a half miles away, I was in high school, sporting a pastel-colored poly-blend uniform dress, undoubtedly zoning out in class.

Note

1. *101*, directed by David Dawkins, Chris Hegedus, and D. A. Pennebaker. (1989; New York: Sony Music Entertainment, 2003), DVD.

1

Got Sort-of Live if You Want It!

Roll the Tape

The live album occupies a special place in the taxonomy of rock 'n roll. It serves several purposes—providing an early or mid-career greatest hits, introducing new fans to the sound. Live albums can animate songs and change a band's fortunes—think *Cheap Trick Live at Budokan* or *KISS Alive*!

The live album, above all, announces in a voice raw and cracked from rocking so hard: We have arrived.

There's a kind of prestige there, a macho demonstration that you can "bring it" in a purely physical way. Hitting drums with sticks, plucking guitar strings—you know, *rocking*— without all that candy-ass studio mumbo-jumbo. Just dudes creating sound by transferring energy from one thing to another right before your eyes and ears.

A live rock album serves as proof of authenticity.

What, then, is a live album made by an electronic band?

DM's 1989 *101* brings another factor to the fore: it's a thundering stadium-sized assertion that the band are not merely synth-playing milquetoasts; laughable, limpid button-pushers who purvey plink-plonky dirges. *101* insists that DM can and will rock you, no guitars required.

101 also serves as a transitional piece between their dues-paying semi-obscurity (in the United States) to arena-straddling, masterpiece-creating, masses-pleasing chartlords. Providing "banger" versions of their career to date, it's a peppery intro to their oeuvre. To this day, *101* continues to serve as a starter kit for DM beginners—that is, a literal Depeche Mode 101 class for generations of DM freshpeople.

The band couldn't have overlooked the live album prestige factor. When announcing "A Concert for the Masses," where *101* was recorded, band member Wilder noted that the concert, held at the Rose Bowl in Pasadena, California, would be the "largest and most prestigious" that the band had yet played.

The concert was hosted by KROQ, a radio station that consciously avoided guitars for most of the 1980s, believing them to reek of dinosaurs and troglodytes—everything KROQ was not.

DM were never shy about using tapes to augment their sound. In early performances, the reel-to-reel, taking the place of a drummer, sat right in the middle of the stage. *101* is also the name of a documentary made by D. A. Pennebaker, which provided some glimpses into DM's touring life, tailed a busload of fans and culminated at the Rose Bowl show, where the band had two tape machines going (in case one failed). As the lads left the dressing room to go onstage, someone yelled, "Roll the tape!"

From Middling to Bangers

I asked Daniel Bukszpan, author of *The Encyclopedia of Heavy Metal* and *The Encyclopedia of New Wave*, what makes for a good live album.[1]

"My take is that a good live album offers something beyond the songs as we know them already," he said.

I noted that, while DM's drum tapes don't allow for "jamming" (a prominent feature of many live albums), the song arrangements are different and more dynamic, and the music that is played live has a different feel than the studio stuff. I added that a few middling tracks become total bangers when they are played live.

"A good live album should transform all that is middling to 'banger' status."

By this metric (and any other, frankly), *101* is a great live album.

Ironically, DM's success helped usher in the era of "alternative rock," which was about as rockist as it gets, all crunchy guitars, growly vocals, and sweaty, hairy men in indifferent clothing. Indeed, indifferent clothing will themselves catch grunge fever and go all rawk. But more about that later.

"Rock musicians say you can't express yourself with a synthesizer. Soulless is the word. But what is there in whacking a guitar? Every heavy metal riff is near enough the same anyway."[2]

Martin Gore, November 1981

The Boys from Basildon

DM began in 1980 with Vince Clarke, Fletcher, Gore, and Gahan, who were first called Composition of Sound. Clarke and Fletcher had done some time in a Christian group called Boys Brigade singing folk tunes and trying to convert people, and Fletcher and Gore attended school together. They had formed a guitar/bass/keyboard trio; after overhearing Gahan singing David Bowie's "Heroes" he became the singer and the band went electronic. Synths were cheaper and more versatile and allowed them to practice quietly, wearing headphones.[3]

They are frequently asked, to this day about the meaning of their name. "Depeche Mode" came from something Gahan saw in a French magazine during his tenure as a window dresser. It means something like "fashion bulletin"—that is, it has nothing to do with the contents of the group. They pronounced it Day-pesh-ay Mode at first, for a little extra flair.[4]

Once, I heard an advertising person say, "Words are merely a vessel we pour meaning into," referring to a campaign that had me furrowing my brow. That has haunted me ever since. If that's true, does that mean that my entire lifetime of using words to express complex ideas and, well, create art, was but a sham? If words have no meaning, can there be any truth? The mirror crack'd in front of me.

But I was just being too literal about a tagline and thinking that the words meant what they actually meant. In retrospect, perhaps I wouldn't have stood there blinking, turning gray and questioning my life path if she had said, "Kinda like band names? You know: Echo and the Bunnymen, Paper Lace, Supertramp."

I would have nodded and added, "Oh right. Sorta like Duran Duran, REO Speedwagon, the Chocolate Watchband." Not that big of a deal.

I'm sure it's exhausting at this point, guys, so if anyone asks you what Depeche Mode means, just hit 'em with "Words are a vessel that we pour meaning into." Because a group of lads from Basildon are about the least Frenchy thing one could imagine.

The *101* documentary shows the lads backstage in their dressing room. Their flight cases are stenciled on the side "Depeche Mode, Basildon, Essex." Their short Twitter bio reads "From beginnings in Basildon …"

Basildon looms large in the DM legend. Richard Blade, the legendary KROQ jock, always said, "It's the Boys from Basildon!" every time DM came on, which was often. I never heard him blare "It's the Boys from Crawley!" every time he played a Cure song. No, DM were always the Boys from Basildon. Having no idea where Basildon was, I assumed it was sinister and that Richard was playing off the title of "The Boys from Brazil," an Ira Levin novel about Nazis hiding in South America and their sinister Nazi breeding scheme. Put together with some of the socialist/Nazi-lite imagery they liked to play with and lyrics about death being everywhere, it made sense.

Basildon was a New Town constructed on London's outskirts after the Second World War. The new towns were built to house factory workers and serve as catchment zones for people spilling out of London.

The New Town plan was part "Let's make special places for the little people so we can ship them off and get them out of our hair" and part "But seriously? How can we live better? Let's get radical."

These modern, clean, and artificial cities of the future were built on semi-rural areas housing "hillbilly Cockneys" in cobbled-together shacks in a muddy, swampy area: a kind of "British Mississippi," suggests Simon Spence, in *Just Can't Get Enough: The Making of Depeche Mode*.[5] He posits that DM, the first British group not influenced by American blues, may have invented the Basildon blues, "a modern blues born out of a feral heritage and the hopes and dreams for the New Town and the nightmare reality of becoming the capital city of Chavland."[6] It was where you might get beaten up for wearing nail polish.

Still, Basildon could be a great place to be a kid. There were areas where cars were barred and kids could run around freely. When it was newly built, it had a space-age feeling, with abstract public sculpture and smooth, fresh concrete everywhere. And, because it was in a field of "nothing to do," young people were inspired to do things to entertain themselves. Things like forming bands,[7] making art, becoming involved in political causes, or, say, Christian youth groups.

DM's fellow world-beating musical mopers the Cure originated from another new town, Crawley. Lol Tolhurst, who founded the Cure with Robert Smith, said that he thinks the Cure and DM strike a chord with many young American listeners due to the bands emerging from boring suburbs.[8] Paloma Romero, the drummer from the Slits, changed the name of a song called "Drugtown" to "Newtown" as she was thinking of bored young people in places like Milton Keynes[9] (which had one of the highest suicide rates in the U.K. in the 1980s) or who "take drugs, drive around fast or beat each other up at football matches."

Basically, DM were tagged early on in England as being hopelessly uncool and that stuck really, really hard. Sophia Deboick in *The Quietus*[10] said that Basildon is "a part of England that nobody talks about and which lacks the cache of Joy Division's Manchester …." Rank snobbery, in other words.

Basildon was called "Little Moscow on the Thames" by a Conservative government official[11] because of its great lashings of concrete and origins in avant-garde thinking, both of which are real plusses in my view. Coincidentally, I have written much of this book in a 1974 vintage Brutalist library that has a lot of the same glorious "Let's fuck some shit up and join the future" energy: raw concrete everywhere, slashes of windows and a challenging, unnecessary, three-story ramp leading from the street to the main room. I find it soothing: concrete doesn't pretend to be something that it's not, and I appreciate the hell out of that.

I enjoyed my breaks, eating clementines and smashed crackers and Goldenberg's Peanut Chews in a deserted concrete courtyard where small, single metal chairs surround a mysterious, large wooden disc. It was a big Depeche Mood.

Sure, Basildon could be rough. "The most suave and sophisticated" Mode,[12] according to Neil Tennant of the Pet Shop Boys, then a writer at Smash Hits. Wilder was warned against (a) bringing his photo bag with him and (b) sitting with his legs crossed in Basildon. Appearing to be a "poof" could get your ass kicked tout de suite.

Basildon, in all its glory, provided the backdrop for what Gahan called "a new kind of band from a new kind of town."

The Modefather

When Mute Records honcho Daniel Miller was at art school, a guest lecturer, Rob Geesin, who had recorded Pink Floyd, brought a synthesizer and let the students play with it. "That was a really important moment for me," he said.[13]

In 1978, Miller, then a twenty-seven-year-old film editor living in London with his mother, figured it was now or never if he wanted to make a record. Punk rock was happening and DIY was in, but Miller found the music quite conservative and unimpressive. Relatively cheap synthesizers allowed for homemade recordings; with a second-hand Korg 700S, he wrote and recorded a few songs in his bedroom.

As The Normal, he released his self-produced only single, the landmark "T.V.O.D." with "Warm Leatherette" on the B-side. Inspired by J. D. Ballard's "Crash," in which Miller's, in an arch, eerie, voice, narrates a tale of a car crash … but a sexy one. Jane Suck, a writer at *Sounds Magazine*, obtained a test pressing and named it "Single of the Century.[14] She wasn't wrong. "Warm Leatherette" is timeless and immaculate. Miller made up the name "Mute Records" and put his mother's address on the back of the sleeve. People started mailing him music.

"Warm Leatherette's" sleeve design included the use of Letraset—a primitive form of manual typesetting using scratch-off sheets that captured the DIY spirit of the times. Miller chose a 1931 German typeface that was used for its road signs. Letraset became part of the label's core identity—it also provided its "walking man" logo, featured on every release.[15]

After Miller met Frank Tovey (who called himself Fad Gadget), an experimental electronic musician, he suggested to Tovey that they put out a single, and voila! With a second artist besides Miller himself, Mute Records was officially born.[16]

Miller didn't create any more music as The Normal, but he did invent an imaginary band called Silicon Teens, which was, like The Normal, Miller himself. The Teens, who were named Darryl, Jacki, Paul, and Diane (the man is a genius, right?), had a pretend frontman: Fad Gadget. Silicon Teens' sole album, *Music for Parties*, hit No. 4 on the U.K. indie chart. Which was respectable, but Miller wanted more. "Although Silicon Teens didn't exist, our press release claimed that they were the world's first teenage all-electronic band. That actually hadn't happened yet. But I knew it was going to happen soon."[17]

In rare, spine-tingling circumstances, highly evolved beings can magick up the most remarkable things from the psychoplastic space around them.

One such wizard, Sam Phillips, created Sun Records to record Black artists—to share their music with the world. He produced records for giants such as Ike Turner, B. B. King, and Howlin' Wolf. Unfortunately, there was a ceiling on sales of so-called "race records" due to white folk not feeling comfy buying them. Phillips knew that the interest was there, though, particularly among teens. "They liked the music, but they weren't sure whether they ought to like it or not," he said.[18] He was really most interested in sharing collective culture. He pondered finding a white man who could bridge the gap—combining the best of Black and white music.

Right on schedule, Elvis Presley walked into his studio.

Decades later, on a different continent, Miller's real-life silicon teens came to life when he saw DM in October 1980, supporting Fad Gadget. The band consisted of teens (and the almost teen) Clarke, twenty, unemployed; singer Gahan, eighteen, college student/trainee window dresser; and keyboardists Martin Gore, nineteen, bank clerk; and Fletcher, nineteen, insurance clerk. "They had a fanbase with them and their fans weren't watching the band," said Miller. "They were just dancing."

Miller, impressed by the quality of their songs, introduced himself, asking the Basildon quartet, "Do you fancy doing a single?" They did (Chiara, 2016). The universe's gears turn in mysterious ways. The Silicon Teens' first single was a cover of "Memphis, Tennessee" by Chuck Berry.

Really Fucking Rocking

In the 1980s, paper publications such as *Melody Maker (MM)* and *New Musical Express (NME)* were the best way to learn about what was going on in the English music scene. At the Waldenbooks at my local mall, I pawed through *MM*s and *NME*s and sometimes even bought one—but they were expensive. I remember reading aloud to a friend that Duran Duran were shooting new videos in Sry Layn-ka. "Sry Layn-ka?" she said, puzzled. "Where's that?" I shrugged. There was no way of knowing other than consulting an encyclopedia, so: we never found out.

In April 1981, the late Seymour Stein, the legendary co-founder of Sire Records who signed, among others, the Ramones, Talking Heads, the (English) Beat, Madness, the Cure, and Echo & the Bunnymen, was sitting in bed, reading a three-week-old copy of *NME*. Stein was the A&R human equivalent of the black-footed cat, the world's deadliest (yet smallest) wildcat. Nocturnal, sure of itself, not a big showy tiger or lion. You'd never see that cat coming until it was too late.

An article caught Stein's eye about a new band, Depeche Mode, who were being produced by Daniel Miller. Stein thought Miller was brilliant and had extremely good taste. He had previously acquired The Normal's single and the Silicon Teens album and released them in the United States.[19]

Stein discovered that DM were playing the next day at a nightclub in Essex. He booked an expensive trip on the Concorde, a then-popular supersonic airplane that made it from NYC to London in mere hours. Due to its cost, the glamorous Concorde, with its singular turned-down beak, belonged in the realm of the rich and/or famous. When Boy George needed to get to London from New York to make it to the Band Aid recording session on time, he took the Concorde.[20] Paul McCartney was known to break out his guitar on flights and play a few tunes.[21] When Phil Collins needed to make it to both Live Aid sites—the Concorde was there. It hit a James-Bondian Mach 2 as it flew 11 miles from the Earth.[22]

Stein's socks were knocked off and he decided to sign DM to Sire. They were the first electronic band that "fucking rocked," he said (Spence, 21).

TV and NYC

DM's first single, "Dreaming of Me," released in February 1981, reached No. 57 on the UK charts—a promising beginning indeed. Their second single, "New Life," reached No. 11, earning them an invitation to perform it on *Top of the Pops* (*TOTP*), a weekly show on the BBC that featured musical acts miming a song. *TOTP*, watched by the nation each week, was an institution—a sign that you had made it. The lads memorably rode the train to the BBC's London studio schlepping their synths under their arms.

The band seems as surprised as anyone that they have found themselves on *TOTP*. This performance is, well, goofy.[23] No one's really sure what they're doing. Gahan has a new-wave bouffant flopping down over one eye and is wearing a poufy pale-orange blouse and leather pants tucked into his boots. As usual, he's giving it his all. Fletcher is awkward in a graphic T-shirt and leather pants, dancing behind his synth. Clarke and Gore are little blond twins in a leather jacket (Clarke) and what appears to be a sheer shirt with bondage overalls (Gore). There's an animated green sine wave superimposed over them, emphasizing their digital-ness. Nice touch, BBC of yore.

This performance seems like it's in a high school lipsync contest. These are cool guys and they are crushing the competition, which includes a pretend Human League (with admittedly, a good Joanne and Susan). You never really noticed Andy Fletcher before? But "He's actually kind of cute," you whisper to a friend.

Fletcher and Gore reported to their jobs the next morning. Soon enough, they quit and committed to life as full-time musicians.

Their third single, released on September 8, 1981, "Just Can't Get Enough," took them to No. 8.

DM played their first concert in the United States on January 22, 1982. Because they had done *TOTP* the day before, the boys arrived via—you guessed it—Concorde.

In the *New York Times*, Stephen Holden[24] described their performance at the Ritz: "Consisting of four young men, three synthesizers and a tape recorder playing prerecorded rhythm tracks, Depeche Mode makes gloomy merry-go-round music with a danceable beat."

Six years later, this group, in the exact same formation, rocked approximately 60,000 people at the Rose Bowl at "A Concert for the Masses."

Holden said that, as compared to the "expressive" music by Giorgio Moroder, Abba, Gary Numan, and Kraftwerk, "Depeche Mode offered only a new flavor of bubblegum." He wasn't wrong there; save for "Tora! Tora! Tora!" written by Gore—a song about a historical event: the bombing of

Pearl Harbor and the namesake film that depicts it. It ends with a haunting refrain: "I played an American," the rest of the songs were pure Clarke—sugary confections he liked to call "Ultra Pop," which wasn't a bad thing and not unexpressive.

A few of DM's girlfriends began a newsletter[25] to send to fans late in 1980. A one-sided typed sheet, it was mostly an order form for merchandise, but also kept fans up to date. Issue #2, (January 1981) had this item:

Depeche Mode News[26]

Vince Clarke has left DEPECHE MODE leaving Gahan, Gore and Andy to continue as a three-piece. The reason for leaving is that he wishes to concentrate on being simply a songwriter.

However, the band will still use his songs and he will be replaced for live appearances.

Notes

1. Daniel Bukszpan, direct message to author, May 23, 2021

2. Kory Grow, "Are Depeche Mode Metal's Biggest Secret Influence?" *Rolling Stone*, August 11, 2015. https://www.rollingstone.com/music/music-features/are-depeche-mode-metals-biggest-secret-influence-56191/

3. *101*, 1989.

4. Betty Page, "Depeche Mode: Depeche Guevara," *Sounds*, June, 1981. www.rocksbackpages.com/Library/Article/depeche-mode-depeche-guevara

5. Simon Spence, *Just Can't Get Enough: The Making of Depeche Mode.* (London: Jawbone Press, 2012), 32.

6. Ibid., 33.

7. *New Town Utopia,* directed by Christopher Ian Smith. (Seattle: Amazon, 2018) https://www.amazon.com/sk=new+town+utopia&crid=2MDA78H3OPXC6&sprefix=new+town+ut%2Caps%2C158&ref=nb_sb_ss_ts-doa-p_1_11

8. Ron Hart, "How America Fell in Love with the Cure," *Observer*, May 27, 2017. https://observer.com/2017/05/the-cure-kiss-me-kiss-me-kiss-me-album-anniversary-review-lol-tolhurst/

9. Viv Albertine, *Clothes, Clothes, Clothes. Music, Music, Music. Boys, Boys, Boys.: A Memoir.* (United Kingdom: St. Martin's Publishing Group, 2014), 217.

10. Sophie Deboick, "Depeche Mode & the Essex New Town," *The Quietus*, October 12, 2011. https://thequietus.com/articles/07165-basildon-speak-spell

11. Tim Burrows, "The Invention of Essex: How a County Became a Caricature," *The Guardian*, June 27, 2019. https://www.theguardian.com/news/2019/jun/27/the-invention-of-essex-how-a-county-became-a-caricature

12. Neil Tennant, "Depeche Mode: Strange but True," *Smash Hits*, November 22–December 5, 1984. https://archive.org/details/smash-hits-22-november-5-december-1984/mode/2up

13. Terry Burrows and Daniel Miller, *Mute: A Visual Document: From 1978–Tomorrow.* (New York: Thames & Hudson, 2017), 30.

14. Yael Chiara, "Discovering Depeche Mode: Interview with Daniel Miller of Mute Records," *Medium*, September 7, 2016. https://medium.com/cuepoint/discovering-depeche-mode-interview-with-daniel-miller-of-mute-records-484bf6eb795d

15. Burrows and Miller, 32.

16. Ibid.

17. Ibid., 51.

18. Jon Garelick, "Rock's Visionary," *Boston Phoenix*, August 8 - 14, 2003. https://bostonphoenix.com/boston/news_features/this_just_in/documents/03073671.a

19. Seymour Stein with Gareth Murphy, *Siren Song*. (New York: St. Martin's Press, 2018), 194.

20. Jake Rossen, "Band Aid: The Charitable—and Controversial—History of 'Do They Know It's Christmas?'" *Mental Floss,* December 13, 2019. https://www.mentalfloss.com/article/610472/do-they-know-its-christmas-band-aid-song-history

21. Michael Kaplan, "Fast Days on the Concorde: Rock Stars, Wine & the '11-Mile-High Club'," *New York Post,* June 15, 2015. https://nypost.com/2019/06/15/fast-days-on-the-concorde-rock-stars-wine-the-11-mile-high-club/

22. Annie Zaleski, "35 Years Ago: Phil Collins Becomes Live Aid's Transcontinental MVP," *Ultimate Classic Rock,* July 13, 2015. https://ultimateclassicrock.com/phil-collins-live-aid/

23. Depeche Mode, "New Life," June 25, 1981, video. https://www.youtube.com/watch?v=sxi6WZ0sFUY

24. Stephen Holden, "Pop: Depeche Mode at Ritz," *New York Times,* January 28, 1982. https://www.nytimes.com/1982/01/28/arts/pop-depeche-mode-at-ritz.html

25. Depeche Mode Information Service, "January 1982 Newsletter." https://dmlive.wiki/wiki/Depeche_Mode_ Information_Service_January_1982_newsletter

26. Depeche Mode Information Service, "Newsletter," January 1982. https://dmlive.wiki/wiki/Depeche_Mode_Information_ Service_January_1982_newsletter

2

Is "Music" Electric?

Synths may bring to mind cool, robotic European figures: Nick Rhodes pouting in a jumpsuit. However, the first major electronic musical instrument, the Telharmonium or Dynamophone, wasn't sleek or chic. Invented by Thaddeus Cahill, the Telharmonium was about 60 feet long (picture four standard-sized sedans lined up end to end) and weighed 200 tons (400,000 pounds, or about the weight of the Statue of Liberty).[1] The instrument used a system of electromechanical tone generators to create a wide range of musical tones and was a bargain at $200,000. It was intended to broadcast music via telephone to homes and businesses.[2] This was the first realization of "music from a distance," anticipating broadcast radio, Internet streaming, Muzak, and network music, according to Nick Collins, Margaret Schedel and Scott Wilson in *Electronic Music*.[3]

More instruments followed, including the theremin, which used no keyboard. It generated electrical fields that altered pitch and amplitude according to a person's hand movements, which appeared to be conducting an invisible orchestra. Futurists rejected traditional music and promoted the use of industrial plants, trains, automobiles, and so forth. In *The Art of Noises*, Luigi Rossalo recommended that "We must fix the pitch and irregulate the harmonics and rhythms of these extraordinarily varied sounds."[4] I yell through time: "Hang on, Luigi! The E-mu Emulator is just around the corner!"

The Hammond organ, invented in 1935, was the first electrical keyboard instrument that achieved mass use— replacing reed organs in churches and taking its place in parlors, capable of a not-too-shabby 253,000,00 tone combinations.[5] In the late 1930s, American composer John Cage advocated the use of new instruments to produce new sounds. His Imaginary Landscape No. 3 included tin cans, frequency oscillators, buzzer, and an amplified coil of wire.[6]

After the Second World War, two broadcasting networks in France and Germany squared off in a "second Cold War" of electronic music with Radiodiffusion Television Francaise-based musique concrete movement and Norwestdeutscher Rundfunk-based elektronishe Musik movement.[7] In short, the French preferred to manipulate real-world sounds such as voices, instruments, boats, pots and pans, and so forth. The Germans preferred electronically generated sounds.

More radio studios followed suit in countries including Poland, Denmark, Japan, and England where the BBC started its Radiophonic Workshop, which focused on providing sound effects and music for its radio and television productions. Nonetheless, the Workshop provided space for Daphne Oram and Delia Derbyshire to experiment and compose.[8]

In 1958, more than two million people encountered composer Edgard Varèse's "Poème électronique," a multimedia installation at the World Fair in Brussels.[9]

The piece was incredibly complex and required an on-site team, and a variety of sounds, both electronic and organic broadcast through 350 loudspeakers.[10]

Moving right along, electronic music began to appear in the *Doctor Who* theme, the solo in Del Shannon's "Runaway," and Wendy Carlos's 1968 smash *Switched-On Bach*. The Beach Boys's theremin-rich freakout, "Good Vibrations," went to No. 1 in the U.K. and the United States in 1966, the same year that the Beatles retreated to the studio.[11] Playing live had become an exercise in futility; no one could hear the music over the wall of screams, the Beatles themselves included. In the studio, they began experimenting with sounds that couldn't be reproduced live, for example, "Tomorrow Never Knows" on *Revolver*, a track built on tape loops. Electronics featured prominently in works by other groups such as Sly and the Family Stone, Roxy Music, and of course, Pink Floyd, who reigned over Friday and Saturday night laser-light shows all over America for decades to come.[12]

Industrial Folk

And then there was Kraftwerk, which translates to "Power Station" in English. Side note: when Duran Duran split into two groups, the synth-heavy Nick-and-Simon fantasia Arcadia and Power Station, with the Taylors, manly guitars, and sweaty, seemingly ancient Robert Palmer (only thirty-six at the time, a mere eleven years older than John Taylor!) on vocals. Palmer was an inexplicable addition to the greater Duran Duran universe, a relic of an unknown past, a disturbing uncle who thought of himself as a sex machine, like greasy-haired Bryan Ferry, who "danced" without ever moving his feet. These rock 'n roll survivors who triumphed anew in the 1980s baffled American children unfamiliar with their earlier works. Power Station named themselves after a New York recording studio but did they also realize that they were taking the name of the standard-bearing Teutonic synth combo?

Kraftwerk is the epitome's epitome of "European" synth music. In 1970, Kraftwerk's founders, Ralf Hutter and Florian Schneider, met at a music conservatory. They were playing at a high level that required hours of repetitive practice every day. They decided to switch to synthesizers. Because synths were easy to play, Hutter and Schneider had more time to focus on structuring the music. Indeed, they believed that synthesizers humanize music instead of making it more sterile because songwriters didn't have to spend so much time on technique.[13]

In 1975, Kraftwerk brought their "industrial folk music" to the Liverpool Empire. In the audience was Andy McCluskey, who went on to form Orchestral Manoeuvres in the Dark. The concert blew McCluskey's mind.[14] A BBC segment at the time notes that the group had just jettisoned its last recognizable instrument, a violin, the previous year, and now used nothing but electronic instruments—keyboards, control panels, and two electronic drum sets, which look like giant aluminum foil-covered Lego pieces.[15]

Something remarkable happened in 1975 in the United States. On May 3, Kraftwerk's "Autobahn" went to number twenty-five on the Billboard U.S. chart.[16] The zesty, bracing "Autobahn" was preceded in the chart by a ton of songs that would fit nicely on a *Soundtrack for Crying* compilation album, ideal for sobbing in a beanbag or behind the wheel of a station wagon while sporting gigantic sunglasses.

"Autobahn" was also the only entry on the chart not crafted from blues-based rock'n'roll. Some groups in the 1–24 slots include the Carpenters, Paul Anka, Al Green, Minnie Riperton, Earth, Wind, and Fire, Queen, Grand Funk Railroad, John Lennon, and Elton John, whose Philadelphia Freedom coincidentally vibed with the nation's coast-to-coast rolling freakout over the upcoming Bicentennial in 1976.

I imagine Kraftwerk's incursion was a small triumph for (a) avant-garde music fans jamming out for once in the car and/or (b) lovers of 70s-style "European" class (see: Perrier, BMWs, Brie, the Concorde, yogurt).

Opening with a sampled car engine sound, "Autobahn's" full twenty-two-minute ride is *Discreet Music*'s "fun" friend. It's delightful, full of lively synth sounds and cool, refreshing, electronically modulated vocals. I can't help but be reminded of an Austrian exchange student who stayed with some family friends in the mid-1980s. The Mitteleuropean lad, clad in "American Levi's," spent the majority of his time smoking hash and playing games on an Apple IIe while listening to Kraftwerk nonstop. I didn't get it at the time, but looking back? Dang, that kid knew how to live.

Stop. Disco!

Two years later, Donna Summer scorched the world with "I Feel Love," which Giorgio Moroder cooked up on a Moog. It caused Brian Eno to freak out during the *Low* sessions, saying it was "going to change the sound of music for the next 15 years."[17] America then experienced a battle royale between denim and Lurex. Disco, much of it synth-heavy, captured the hearts and feet of the nation. People—nay, Americans—were *dancing*.

Meanwhile, rock fans, feeling threatened by everything but especially things that emanated from black and/or gay urban culture, embraced the "Disco Sucks!" movement.

At "Disco Demolition Night" at a 1979 Chicago White Sox home game where disco albums were blown up between games in a double-header, disco-haters wilded out, stormed the field, set fires, chucked beer bottles and LPs, and crushed the batting cage. Riot police were called in to quell the outburst but the field was ruined and the second game was canceled.[18]

A stop sign near my house had been defaced by someone who wrote "DISCO" under "STOP." As someone who had installed a blinking Christmas light in my room so that my best friend and I could dance our little hearts out to repeated plays of Summer's "On the Radio," in a proper disco environment, I didn't get the message. Some dude with a wispy mustache and a face full of acne, no doubt, was so infuriated by the existence of fun music and joy that he was moved to deface public property, stating that disco itself should be stopped because he didn't like it.

I thought the graffito meant: "Stop. Disco!"—as in, "Take a moment out of your day to do a few John Travolta moves while you pause at this intersection."

Unfortunately, the rock versus disco conflict in all its myriad versions still runs deep in the United States. Decades after the disco-haters' bonfire, white American citizens attacked the Capitol, breaking windows, smearing feces, and brutally injuring and killing people in the name of a racist, sexist, homophobic, ignorance-promoting asshole, the biggest "Disco Sucks" rally in history, a tantrum of imagined persecution by people who got violent because they didn't like the proverbial music of democracy. There wasn't a person among that dirty-jean-clad white- supremacist horde who could dance and that is a fact.

Indeed, they are the same losers who waged war on the United States in the 1860s because they wanted slavery to continue. Unfortunately, while the United States won the war, Uncle Sam flinched when it came time to finish the job post-war, resulting in hundreds of years of violent white grievance.

While disco-haters ran amok, other things were happening on both sides of the Atlantic: Punk and its almost simultaneous successor, post-punk.

It's Not Punk, It's New Wave

Punk rock didn't really catch on in the United States like it did in England—not that the United States wasn't riddled with hardcore bands, but England is a much smaller country and famously receptive to new pop music movements. Also, things were exceptionally bleak in England in the mid to late 1970s; and let's face it: the English have been known to exhibit flair and humor that doesn't quite translate.

America's malaise took on a slightly different hue. That hue was beige. But more about that later.

There was confusion about what "punk" meant in the U.S. Groups like the Police, Blondie, Talking Heads, and the Ramones were called punk. But were they? Was the Clash punk? Who knew? Seymour Stein thought that "punk" had bad connotations in America, anyway, so he laid down a directive in 1977 to everyone involved in music—"every program director, plugger and hippie jock"—that Talking Heads, et. al., weren't "punk." They were "new wave."[19]

Before I heard them, I thought that the Sex Pistols were going to blow my mind with some incredible chaos I hadn't heard before. I mean, they were the SEX PISTOLS. Yikes!

It was like biting into what appeared to be a delicious chocolate Easter bunny, only to find that it was hollow and cheap, waxy. The Sex Pistols were just rock. Upbeat rock with Englishy, yell-y vocals. Cheerful. One could easily imagine a group of Muppets in felt Mohawks doing their own version of "Anarchy in the U.K.," which would probably be "Anarchy in the Alphabet," detailing the adventures of letters defying their proper place in their twenty-six-slot hierarchy.

If there were honesty in packaging, the Sex Pistols would have been called "The Shouty Monkees."

Rock had, for some, reached a dead end. Guitars, and cock rock, seemed passé. Gary Numan was all set to record a punk album with his band, Tubeway Army, when, in the studio, he encountered a synth and began noodling around on it.[20] Soon enough, he dyed his natural blond hair black, became a white-faced android, and blew England's mind with an unsettling appearance on Top of the Pops. Tubeway Army's album, *Replicas*, featured a song about a robot prostitute called "Are 'Friends' Electric?" Many miles away in Minneapolis, Prince (His Purple Highness) picked up what Gary was putting down, calling Numan a "genius" and saying that *Replicas* was never far from his turntable when he was in junior high.[21]

Numan, unfortunately, couldn't catch a break from the English critics who derided him as a Bowie knockoff. I don't really see it. I think they thought that Numan was uncool, an unforgivable sin. Being named Gary was surely a factor.

All over England, it seemed, young folk were taking synths and going loco with possibilities. Future superstars, including the Human League, the Cure, and Joy Division/New Order began recording classics.

Frame: Broken

After DM's principal songwriter Clarke left one month before their first album, *Speak & Spell*, came out, the band was left at loose ends. Clarke, at twenty-one, earned rock's "Eat a Peach" honor given to those who bid their bands adieu mid-song. Clarke resigned after DM's three hit singles. Neil Young, of course, bailed on Stephen Stills via telegram in the middle of a tour, telling him to munch the stone fruit. Other awardees include Brian Eno, who noped out of Roxy Music after a minor show kerfuffle, and the entire Police, who, riding high on their blockbuster fifth album, *Synchronicity*, didn't officially break up, but sorta did.

A photo from the immediate post-Clarke era shows Gore, Gahan, and Fletcher looking a little bit bereft yet resolute in matching sweaters. Gore stepped up to take on the challenge of songwriting. And DM went from Ultra Pop to something else entirely.

Clarke wrote lyrics to fit the music, resulting in such gems as: "Timing reason, understanding/Like association hall." Clarke's lyrics are exactly like the lyrics I frequently hear. For example, until quite recently I thought that the refrain of Thomas Dolby's "Europa and the Pirate Twins" was "We'll meet in Cairo tombs again, Europa," instead of (duh) "We'll be the pirate twins again, Europa." In "Wrapped Around Your Finger" by the Police, I thought that Sting was saying "Hidden the casbah you will fashion linger," instead of "Hypnotized by you if I should linger."

Clarke's departure seemed catastrophic at the time and the music press was agog with this development, even though being left high and dry without the band's scribe was indeed a predicament. Their remarkable success came from three Clarke-penned singles.

A photo from the immediate post-Clarke era shows Gore, Gahan, and Fletcher looking a little bit bereft in matching sweaters.

They didn't let Clarke's departure break their stride, though. In true, dogged Basildon fashion, they just kept going. Gore, who had contributed "Tora! Tora! Tora!" and the instrumental "Big Muff" to *Speak & Spell*, stepped into the void and, for decades to come, penned monster after monster.

A Broken Frame, their next album, isn't well-loved by the band or fans, but it holds a special place in my heart. A blend of *Speak & Spell*-style sugar-glazed songs such as "A Photograph of You" and "The Meaning of Love," and moodier, odder, and sadder songs such as the glorious "Leave in Silence," "The Sun and the Rainfall," and the delightfully weird "Monument," it may seem uneven or awkward. However, as a young teen, it made perfect sense.

Depeche Comes Alive!

During one of my many adult no-sleep jags, I delved deeply into DM's oeuvre, including a recording of a 1982 concert at the Hammersmith Apollo. We see the lads in the same grouping they will take to the Rose Bowl: a singer, three synth players, and a tape machine. The circle is, once again, complete.

When I look at live footage of post-Clarke DM, I get the same retroactive incipient thrills as when I view black-and-white footage of an early Beatles TV appearance, all glossy hair and big smiles. This DM footage takes on the significance of lore. Are DM the electronic Beatles? It's a fair question. Draw your own conclusion.

Alan Wilder, a classically trained musician and old hand in the recording studio, answered an ad in *Melody Maker* for a band looking for a keyboardist "under 21." Wilder fibbed about his age but blew the Modes away with his ability to play whatever they asked him to—and sing too.

He didn't become a full member of DM right away, though. The three wanted to put out an album on their own before expanding to four. However, Wilder began to tour with the band and appeared in the "See You" and "Meaning of Love" videos.

Tall, pale Fletcher, whose look here is "new wave android in earth tones," stares vacantly ahead, plunking a few keys, his face expressionless. He represents the melding of man and machine, the very personification of DM. His outfit—a leaf-green shirt, brown paper-bag waisted pants, and a jaunty cap, emphasizes his "Hobbot" vibe.

Fletcher's real job was to handle stuff for the group, who manage themselves, but his *real* real job was to be there for his best mate, reticent, sensitive Gore, who needed a dedicated emotional support human to help him withstand the pressure of being in a successful electronic pop combo.

In the annals of taking a ride with one's best friend, Fletcher was perhaps the greatest of all time.

On the next synth over, cute lil' punkin and genius songwriter Gore sports a frothy head of thick blond curls, wispy facial hair, and a denim vest that appears to be lined with shearling. Inscrutable but cuddly, he resembles a gentle carny who specializes in church festivals, and you know what? You're OK with it when he shows up on your doorstep to take your daughter out. It's gotta happen sometime, you reckon. This little guy will treat her with respect and tenderness, then head off to a parish 300 miles to the north, thus freeing her from the burdens of virginity *and* having to be his girlfriend, which wouldn't work out since she's pretty busy with school and choir. Later in DM's career, he'll dress for an entirely different sort of carnival.

Frosty, feline Londoner Wilder is the musical wizard of the bunch, a growing shaper of sonic landscapes. Cool as hell, even at this stage; he's wearing an Eisenhower-length brown leather jacket—black leather is waiting in the wings. Wilder has the enthusiasm of the new guy in the office. He is more animated here than he will be for the next thirteen years onboard the *S.S. Depechia*, breaking out adorably sincere singing faces and boogying smoothly behind the keys.

Gahan enters dancing from the wings, joyful and apple-cheeked, all nose and ears and big brown eyes. He's wearing a plaid flannel shirt tucked into belted, pleated pants, the most cherubic of boys despite having done some time in English juvie. Gahan opens his mouth, and his booming baritone takes center stage. When he's not singing, he's dancing, clapping, engaging the audience however he can. It's hard to discern, but there's a ropy rock legend in the making under all that baby fat and wonder.

A Broken Frame is an odd record for sure—Gore reached into his own personal backlog to pull out sweet teenage numbers as "A Photograph of You," "See You," and "The Meaning of Love." These songs are underrated in my opinion. Although perky and poppy, they all have a melancholy streak under all that candy. The narrator of "See You" is desperate to see his former squeeze five years after their parting, promising to try not to touch, kiss, or hold her. In fact, she can keep him physically away from her if she doesn't trust him not to touch her. Weirdly, he says he knows it's been five years and a lot can change in that time, but that people are "basically the same"—a bit of Gore humor.

If that's true, then whatever caused her to break up with him hasn't changed at all. Whatever it was that makes him "swear" he won't touch her—still the same.

I also like "The Meaning of Love." It's a classic topic for a pop song—what is this thing we call "love?" The narrator is diligent in his search for answers. He reads more than 100 books, asks his friends (who think he's lost his mind) and finally, entreats the Lord for an answer. The closest he can get to a definition is that love is something like "wanting a scar"—a bit dour, that, but a preview of the Depeche Mood.

The rest of the album gives bigger clues about the direction DM will go. That is: minor key. Gore thought that minor keys "were more realistic" anyway. The album kicks off with the stunning "Leave in Silence," which spoke to me. Perhaps it refers to Clarke's departure.

"Monument" is about a group effort to build something out of stone—seemingly unassailable—yet it crumbles after the last stone is placed. "My monument/it fell down." This could surely describe the monument that was DM, original version—and the unexpected crumbling of the group just as the monument was completed (several weeks from the first album's release). There's no resolution—just the scattered bricks.

"My Secret Garden" is the type of track that didn't make it to 101's golden California shores. Synth-heavy, with long vocal-less sections, it's haunting and gentle. Gore's lyrics are straightforward, yet open to interpretation as Gore intends.

The album closes with the beautiful "The Sun and the Rainfall." Relationships, like the weather, are unpredictable—

"Things must change/we must rearrange them." Better to do that than keep on playing the same old games. Gore, Fletcher, and Gahan surely knew this, adapted and decided to rearrange things, surfing the tides of life's vicissitudes.

Additionally, *A Broken Frame*'s sleeve is a no-kidding masterpiece and made me feel quite sophisticated when I studied it. Brian Griffin's photo of a peasant woman scything grains in a field is breathtaking, miraculous in its unmanipulated state. Even the title's calligraphy soothed my little soul. Here was something, it said, that is built to last.

As for Clarke, he went off with singer Alison Moyet, an old schoolmate of Andy and Gore, to form another successful group, Yaz (Yazoo in England). Clarke had apparently realized he didn't need to compromise—he could do it on his own.

Notes

1. Peter Manning, *Electronic and Computer Music,* 4th ed. (New York: Oxford University Press, 2013), 3.

2. Ibid., 4.

3. Nick Collins, Margaret Schedel, and Scott Wilson, *Electronic Music.* (Cambridge, Cambridge University Press, 2013), 31.

4. Ibid., 140.

5. Ibid., 41.

6. Manning, *Electronic Music,* 16.

7. Collins, Schedel, and Wilson, *Electronic Music,* 50.

8. Ibid., 59.

9. Ibid., 61.

10. Ibid.

11. Ibid., 84.

12. Ibid.

13. J.D. Considine, "Depeche Mode: Rooted in Rock," *The Baltimore Sun*, May 5, 1988. www.newspapers.com/ image/377877002

14. David Buckley, *Kraftwerk: Publikation.* (London: Omnibus Press, 2015), 81.

15. BBC Archive, "1975: Kraftwerk—Music of the Future?" video, 1.39, September 1975. https://www.youtube.com/ watch?v=Hmu8LL-K3KM

16. "Hot 100," *Billboard*, May 3, 1975. https://www.billboard.com/ charts/hot-100/1975-05-03/

17. Simon Reynolds, "Song from the Future: The Story of Donna Summer and Giorgio Moroder's I Feel Love," *Pitchfork*, June 29, 2017. https://pitchfork.com/features/article/song-from-the-future-the-story-of-donna-summer-and-giorgio-moroders-i-feel-love/

18. Joe Lapointe, "The Night Disco Went Up in Smoke," *New York Times*, July 4, 2009. http://www.nytimes.com/2009/07/05/ sports/baseball/05disco.html

19. Stein with Murphy, *Siren Song: My Life in Music*, 150.

20. BBC, "Synth Britannia, Gary Numan on Discovering Synths," February 17, 2011. video. https://www.bbc.co.uk/ programmes/p00f4cyl

21. Kathleen Johnston, "Gary Numan: 'It Should Be a Criminal Offence for Politicians to Lie to the Public.'" *GQ (British Edition)* (October 23, 2020). https://www.gq-magazine.co.uk/ culture/article/gary-numan-interview

3

It's Hip, It's Totally Hip, It's the Only Thing Happening

One day in 1982, I sat down at my mother's typewriter and made an important list on a piece of fine onionskin paper.

It was called BANDS I HATE.

Unranked, its members included Foreigner, Asia, Journey, the Stones, REO Speedwagon, Eagles, Supertramp, AC/DC, Boston, Van Halen, Rush, Led Zeppelin, The Doors, Steve Miller Band, Pink Floyd, The Who, Genesis, Air Supply, Three Dog Night, etc. Some of them I hated so much they got extra force, nearly breaking through the sheet.

Although there was a lot happening with Talking Heads, Cheap Trick, Blondie, B-52's, etc., America (the country, not the band) was in a bit of a dirty-beige funk in the late 1970s/early 1980s, a miasma of feathered hair, corduroy shorts, and roach clips. Some of us had spent the 1970s listening to Wings (including my small self) because of Paul, but that was a chore at times even for believers. Still, we kept the light on. However, when John Lennon was murdered in 1980, it was official: The Beatles couldn't save us now.

Disco faded from view; the nation was smothered in AOR (Album Oriented Rock), a format that featured the smooth, unsexy corporate rock sounds of artists such as Toto, Styx, Aerosmith, Bob Seger, and Survivor. It was a warm, beige blanket of aural mushroom soup. Years later, my college roommates would confiscate my cassette of Boston's first album because I played it too much, but at the time, I wanted no part of any of that. AOR said "no future" to me far louder than anything the Sex Pistols ever released. It felt like a future of burgundy-colored nylon, velcro on everything and an endless supply of guys named Scott or Rick pretending not to realize a girl is only twelve.

AOR, in short, felt like ripping your exposed, shorts-clad thighs off of hot vinyl bucket seats.

Roq of the '80s

DM's eventual ownership of the greater Los Angeles Metropolitan Area didn't just happen. You can't grow trees on Mars without terraforming it first. Los Angeles had to be primed. The process began in 1979 when Rick Carroll landed at KROQ 106.7 FM in Pasadena, California[1].

KROQ wasn't in the best shape.

KROQ was playing typical rock out of its seedy, run-down studio in sleepy Pasadena. In 1976, the "Mayor of the Sunset Strip" and former owner of "Rodney Bingenheimer's English Disco" began his radio show, "Rodney on the Roq." He was the first to play punk, but his interests were wide-ranging.[2] He broke many bands in the Southland, including

Duran Duran, Van Halen, the Go-Go's and Joan Jett and the Blackhearts.[3] Bingenheimer's y's show ran for more than forty years.

In KROQ's gross, green-carpeted studio, anarchy ruled the day.[4] It was awash in lawsuits and financial woes. Paychecks regularly bounced. By 1978, the station began adding new artists such as Tom Petty, the Ramones, Blondie, and the Tubes, but it didn't change to all "New Music" overnight.

Dusty Street, the first female DJ on the West Coast and a veteran of San Francisco's legendary freeform station KSAN, said, "I was playing Flash in the Pan back to back with AC/DC and then Television. We really weren't 'reborn' at the very beginning, but we were bringing this new quote-unquote punk and new wave music—the Sex Pistols and Gen X and X-Ray Spex and those kinds of bands."[5]

New Wave Top 40

After Carroll's arrival, he installed a format based on the basic top 40 notion pioneered by Todd Storz at KOWH in Omaha in the early 1950s.[6] After implementing Storz's format, KOWH's share of listeners went from 4 percent to 45 percent.[7] He acquired several other stations throughout the United States, which all met with the same stratospheric success.[8] Storz felt that repetition was key to gaining listeners. The number of songs in the "Top 40" was based on the rough number of songs that could be played in a typical three-hour shift.[9]

Along with programming, a key element of Storz's approach was encouraging DJs to lead with their personalities.[10] The hits may have been the same, but each jock was an individual, engaging listeners with their own quirky energy.

By the end of the decade, transistor technology allowed for a huge increase in car radios, and then small, portable transistor radios gave teenagers the ability to listen to music wherever they went. Radio stations took on identities, giving teenagers a sense of belonging. The sheer mass of Baby Boomers combined with teenage tunes on tap provided the optimal conditions for the Beatles to arrive and rule, setting off the rock 'n roll explosion of the 1960s.

Carroll's format was called "Roq of the 80s." He sensed that there was an audience who had grown tired of the same old 1970s stuff—primarily teenagers and young adults who weren't being served otherwise.

Carroll created pie charts (or "hot clocks") for the jocks. Each wedge had a list of songs. "You could choose any one of those songs and then you'd go to the next piece and choose from Los Lobos and Ian Dury and the Stones and then move on to the next piece. So, it would sound different for whoever was putting it together," said April Whitney,[11] who began at KROQ in 1978 as an intern and graduated to jockhood in '78. "Richard (Blade) might put it together very differently than say, Dusty (Street) or I might put it together." Carroll wasn't using research to choose the songs. He operated on instinct.

Carroll's ideas were met with some resistance by the KROQ jocks, who were used to doing as they pleased. "All hell broke loose," he said. "The jocks were outside picketing two days after I arrived." A compromise was reached—they would try to do things his way, and he would listen to their input.[12]

The jocks had one pick per hour when they could choose anything they wanted to play— "something weird, something not on the playlist or something you might want to give more attention to," said Whitney. "I always tried to give local or struggling, unsigned bands a chance. They didn't always do well, but sometimes they took off."

The jocks were also encouraged to inject their personalities into the proceedings. Carroll wanted it to sound "like there was always a party going on." Listeners were receptive. KROQ's ratings grew as did its influence.

Angelenos were listening. On August 31, 1980, reader Sari Adel[13] wrote a letter to the *L.A. Times* in response to an article about rock standby KMET's which cited it as a "progressive" station. Adel took umbrage. KMET, with its pounding rock, was hardly progressive but you know who was? KROQ, which was left out of the article. She said that KROQ has been playing new bands for years, and the station had been gaining listeners. Furthermore, some of KROQ's featured bands, including Talking Heads, the B-52's, the Clash and the Pretenders, were starting to be played by other stations. KMET should watch out, she warned: KROQ was coming for them.

In 1981, the Basildon lads reached the ears of Southern California. "I'll tell you how Depeche Mode wound up on KROQ," said Dusty Street. "I had a friend who regularly brought singles over from England. He brought 'Just Can't

Get Enough', and I loved it so much that I trapped the program director in his office and played it for him over and over again until he added it."

That same year, MTV began broadcasting music videos 24/7. Most American artists didn't have any, but guess who did? England, thus heralding the beginning of the Second British Invasion.

Radio, Radio

When I was twelve, I discovered something magical and that was KROQ 106.7. My stereo system consisted of (1) a small AM/FM radio that I "borrowed" from my dad—but he had several. His radios existed for the sole purpose of listening to Vin Scully's coverage of Dodger games (sponsored by Faaarmer John!) (2) a rectangular tape recorder that I used to tape stuff off of the radio and TV by holding it up to the source (3) a yellow 1970s-era record player with a clamshell lid.

I came to KROQ for "Stray Cat Strut" by the Stray Cats and stayed for the Go-Go's, "Rock the Casbah" by the Clash (seemed totally badass) and, harkening back to the Iran hostage crisis—"I Ran" by a Flock of Seagulls.

At 1982's New Music Seminar in New York City, Arista president Clive Davis lamented fusty rock radio —"Why is AOR closer to Lawrence Welk than Pac-Man?" He pointed to KROQ as leading the way in this new-music, new-wave era. People needed to get on board before they drowned, sunk by AOR, he warned. "The floodgates will open. The tides can't be stemmed."[14]

Of course, there are always people who complain that something isn't cool enough or is too commercial for their taste. From the get-go, people complained that KROQ was too commercial and didn't play enough punk. However, that same year, a member of Chicago punk band the Effigies, interviewed in Southern California's punk rock fanzine, Flipside, in 1982, said that Chicago radio sucked and he couldn't believe it when people complained about KROQ and KNAC—another L.A. station that had taken up the "progressive" music cause. "Black Flag at ten in the morning—what more do you want?"[15] In that issue, Rodney Bingenheimer's Top 20 had Black Flag at No. 1, along with Circle Jerks, Toni Basil, L.A.'s Wasted Youth, Blasters and Christian Death.

In late July 1982, Billboard reported that, according to Capitol Records, when KROQ played Missing Persons, 70,000 copies were sold in the L.A. market.[16]

Informally, Carroll said, KROQ and MTV played about 40 percent of the same artists—those neglected by AOR stations, who were "not serving youth." Additionally, many of KROQ's offerings were danceable—"the new disco format without the backlash."[17]

Second British Invasion

A 1983 article about the Second British Invasion in Rolling Stone talks about the turning of the AOR tide, MTV and Carroll's success at KROQ in the 80s.[18] AOR's "anesthetic formula of corporate-rock snoozers like Journey, mixed in with all the Springsteen-Seger-Petty clones, had worn out its welcome" in the late 1970s. In 1983, AOR's grip on American radio was beginning to loosen as young people sought out different sounds, leaving "yesterday's Big Macs—the Starship and Speedwagon types" unloved by record companies.

DM weren't really part of the "New Pop" or "Second British Invasion" like bands such as Duran Duran, Thompson Twins, Wham!, Culture Club, Spandau Ballet, etc.[19] Notably, Bob Geldof didn't phone them up and tell them to come down to the studio to join the recording of "Do They Know It's Christmas?" the first charity single to raise money for famine in Ethiopia.

Members from Duran Duran, Spandau Ballet, Bananarama, George Michael, and Culture Club did participate, as did Bono, already a Big Music lord who belted out the song's crucial line—thanking God that you're not one of the starving Ethiopians, which was probably meant to say, "Be grateful for what you have," but in the 1980s, seemed more like gloating: "OMG, I'm so, like, grateful that I'm not like, one of those starving people?"

I have a tradition of watching "The Making of Do They Know It's Christmas?" every Christmas Eve. I can quote dialogue. Thinking about DM there makes me giggle. It's fun to imagine Gahan battle it out vocally with ego-rich superhams Simon Le Bon, Sting and Bono. Perhaps Gore would have found himself strumming a guitar in a hallway with Status Quo while Fletcher chatted with everyone. Wilder would have been in the control booth, elbowing Midge Ure out of the way.

Beige Bummers

In the early 1980s, the future arrived and it was cool, metallic, shiny, and not a minute late.

The United States in the 1970s was riding a major, major bummer. Our national pride had been wounded by Watergate, although Nixon was allowed to escape scot-free due to having been elected president, which set a bad precedent. The Vietnam War dragged into 1975.

The powers that be decided that America's bicentennial was just the tonic to lift us out of our doldrums and remember our origin story. White Americans' origin story, that is.

"Groovy Colonial" decor became popular and homes were adorned with pewter pitchers, spindle rockers, and brick hearths. My brothers and I used to take decorative but very real, heavy, long, antique Civil War-era muskets down from their prime spot above our family room fireplace and shoot each other, failing to observe the "treat every gun like it's loaded" rule.

There was a lot of beige, brown, and rust. In Southern California, even the air joined in the earth tones rage. It was a rainbow of tan, ochre and dirty, dirty orange. The air quality was legendarily bad. It was odd: all the TV shows I watched were filmed in SoCal, but I lived there, too, and it wasn't anything like that.

We were cocooned in a hot blanket of brown particulates.

Once, at the National Portrait Gallery in Washington, D.C., my daughter and I were taking a tour through the presidential portraits. When we got to Jimmy Carter, she

screwed up her face and said, "Why is it so *yellow and tan*?"
"It was the late 70s," I said. "Malaise."

The weirdest thing about the 1970s was that we had a drought and energy crisis and adjusted our lives accordingly—turning off the water while we brushed our teeth and fixing all the drips—getting energy-efficient Japanese cars—and were handed meter sticks at school and told that the United States was going to join the rest of the world and measure things in sensible multiples of ten.

However, water-wasting and gas-guzzling came back as soon as they could and everyone forgot about the metric system.

I, like many in my small generational cohort, was left with a strong, lingering feeling that the "authorities" couldn't be trusted, which I believe led to our teenage snark, irony and wearing of black.

Balance: Righted

DM needed a single between *A Broken Frame* and their next album.

That single was "Get the Balance Right!" It was Wilder's first outing as an official member. I don't know why "Balance" is so disliked by DM; it ranks in my top five easily.[20]

Sassy horn-sounding synths issue an opening clarion call to all in earshot: pay attention! No matter how many times I've heard this song I always get this cool, green, minty feeling on the back of my neck when that little counter-melody kicks in. Then it's just pure electro-jamming for 3–15 minutes, depending on which version you're listening to. Typical of Gore's lyrics, they can be interpreted in a variety of ways. It seems rather a practical point of view to me. The world is full of selfish people (including you) and it's hard to know what to do next all the time, really. You're going to have to compromise and lie to get along—just make sure you don't do too much of it, setting yourself up for a fall. Then one of Gore's greatest. "It's almost predictable. Almost."

The outro leaves me bereft. It gives me the same Saturday-at-4 feeling when you've just finished watching *Yellow Submarine*, that you were basically sitting through for the songs and the part at the very end where the Beatles make a quick appearance. It's too brief a glimpse, and when they disappear, you're suddenly aware of the dust motes swirling in the late-afternoon sun and feel abandoned.

Techsplaining

In May 1982, Richard Cromelin, in the L.A. Times, said in a review of the band's show at the Roxy, they certainly weren't trying to hide the fact that they were using a tape as the drummer—the TEAC had its own spotlight—and commended their with spontaneity. With the band locked into a predefined format, it was like watching a repeat of a game when you already know the score.[21]

DM's trusty TEAC and lack of guitars caused American critics to malfunction. It's like America was a Bachman Turner Overdrive-loving old-timey boxy silver robot watching DM perform from behind one-way mirror glass in an experiment, with a patient investigator standing by.

"How is this a rock band? There are no guitars," Ameribot says in a flat robot voice to the investigator.

"That's right. They use keyboards."

"Key ... boards?"

"Yes, the instruments that can produce the sounds of a variety of musical instruments and all kinds of other things. You can even add real sounds like fireworks and jackhammers and foosball tables."

"There is no drummer?"

"No, the rhythm section is that tape machine."

The Ameribot, although a machine itself, tries to grok this info. It's too much: smoke starts pouring out of its ears. "Does not compute, does not compute!" it says, rocking from side to side, then blows a fuse and catches on fire.

This happens time and time again, all over the nation, for years to come.

In a segment from a local San Francisco music show in May 1982, Gahan stands next to the TEAC and explains that it provides the rhythm. "We've never had a drummer," he says, smiling. He explains that the band uses the drum tracks from their studio records and jokes that it would be great to have a real drummer but the TEAC probably keeps better time.[22]

Gore says, that while he composes songs on a guitar, the guitar is essentially boring. "You can flange it or put it through an echo or something but it's still basically the same sound," he says. Synths, however, offer infinite sonic possibilities.

He adds that he doesn't like to explain or interpret his songs, another key point in Gore's philosophy, which he'll repeat time and time again. "If you're going to write songs, you might as well try and express them, then leave it up to the imagination of the listener."

"New member Al Wilder" holds forth on "technologically sophisticated computerized keyboards." He's New-Wave professorial in a roomy blazer and high-waisted slacks. He's energized the way people are when they are finally talking to someone who actually gives a fuck, or is pretending to, about the thing they like to do.

"Sometimes it can take a long time to find the sound that you want," he says, standing in front of a synth. "But that's the fun part. When you find it, you can store it in the keyboard."

He demonstrates how you can split the board in two, and plays a bit of "Tora! Tora! Tora!" using a bass sound on one side and a "stringy sound" on the other. He instantly enters the zone, making an exquisite "Hell yeah, I am *jamming* on these keys" face.

Notes

1. Robert Atwan, Barry Orton and William Vesterman, *American Mass Media*. (New York: Random House, 1986), 261.

2. Sharon M. Hannon, *Punks*. (Santa Barbara, CA: Greenwood Press, 2010), 44.

3. "Rodney Bingenheimer," *Wikipedia*, October 15, 2022. https://en.wikipedia.org/wiki/Rodney_Bingenheimer

4. Kate Sullivan, "KROQ: An Oral History," *Los Angeles Magazine,* November, 2001. http://radiohitlist.com/KROQ/KROQ-Kate-Sullivan-Los-Angeles-Magazine.htm

5. Dusty Street, interview by Mary Valle, April 24, 2022.

6. Marc Fisher, *Something in the Air: Radio, Rock and the Revolution That Shaped a Generation.* (New York: Random House, 2007), 9.

7. Ibid., 10.

8. Ibid., 15.

9. Ibid., 16.

10. Ibid., 15.

11. April Whitney, interview by Mary Valle, February 6, 2023.

12. James Brown, "KROQ Comes Up from the Bottom," *Los Angeles Times,* July 12, 1981. https://www.newspapers.com/image/387458132

13. Sari Adel, "Don't Knock ROQ," *Los Angeles Times*, August 31, 1980. https://www.newspapers.com/image/387145526

14. Randal Doane, *Stealing All Transmissions: A Secret History of the Clash.* (Oakland, CA: PM Press, 2014), 153.

15. "The Effigies," *Flipside,* November 30, 1982. https://archive.org/details/Flipside301982/page/n1/mode/2up

16. Douglas E. Hall, "Carroll Consultancy Expands to Expand KROQ Formula," *Billboard,* July 31, 1982. https://books.google.com/books?id=lSQEAAAAMBAJ&pg=PT5&dq=%22Carroll+Consultancy+Moves+to+Expand+KROQ+Formula%22&hl=en&sa=X&ved=2ahUKEwiYoMix5MGCAxW8FlkFHTr0B6kQ6AF6BAgHEAI#v=onepage&q=%22Carroll%20Consultancy%20Moves%20to%20Expand%20KROQ%20Formula%22

17. Ibid.

18. Parke Puterbaugh, "Anglomania: The Second British Invasion," *Rolling Stone,* November 10, 1983. https://www.rollingstone.com/music/music-news/new-wave-1980s-second-british-invasion-52016/3/

19. Theo Cateforis, interview by Mary Valle, April 28, 2021.

20. Spence, *Just Can't Get Enough*, 205.

21. Richard Cromelin, "Depeche Mode and Tape at the Roxy," *Los Angeles Times,* May 18, 1982. https://www.newspapers.com/image/388999007

22. VideowestTV, "Videowest—Depeche Mode," March 29, 1983, video, 4:28. https://www.youtube.com/watch?v=2vHqNtpQtIU.

4

Found Sounds

Roq'in America

In August 1982, the *L.A. Times* reported that "wizard" Rick Carroll, whose new wave/Top 40 music format had "been the talk of the music business" for months, started a consultancy to bring his "Roq of the 80s" format to other stations, but was beaten to the punch by WLIR in New York. WLIR, which would become DM's other stronghold in the United States, had gone ahead and installed a "virtual replica" of KROQ's format. I.e.? Totally ripped them off.[1]

A "local promotion man" noted that the station's program director had been firmly against new wave, so his change of heart might mean that "new music" was going to stick around—if it was successful in Long Island, it might have a chance in other places, too.

Meanwhile, KROQ's influence continued to grow. Carroll was focused on teens, with an eye toward capturing them young and keeping them for years. The station's playlist contained such saucy, fresh anthems as Soft Cell's "Sex Dwarf," which came in at No. 3 on its annual year-end top 106.7 songs of the year, "Blue Spark" by X (No. 10), and "Walking in L.A." by Missing Persons (No. 11).

Feeling Teutonic

After recording their third album, *Construction Time Again,* at electronic music pioneer John Foxx's studio, DM decamped to Berlin's famed Hansa studios, where David Bowie made a great deal of his "Berlin trilogy," to mix their third album, Gareth Jones, who engineered the album, had just worked with industrial-music pioneers Einstürzende Neubauten and wasn't interested in working with DM. He thought they were too slight, too poppy. However, encouraged by Foxx, Jones met the band, liked them, and decided to take them on.[2]

Berlin was a *thing.* David Bowie, after a chaotic spell in Los Angeles, was newly enthusiastic about groups such as Neu!, Kraftwerk, and Brian Eno's increasingly instrumental stylings. Bowie had also been doing "America" for several years and was looking to get back to Europe. Indeed, his retreat to Berlin was also intended as an opportunity to "get clean" after years of cocaine use in the City of Angels where things got exceedingly weird. He had his pool exorcised, for starters.[3]

"What I was passionate about in relation to Kraftwerk was their singular determination to stand apart from stereotypical American chord sequences and their wholehearted embrace of a European sensibility," Bowie said.[4]

Moving in a darker direction, *Construction Time Again* marked the first time that DM made extensive use of sampling. Inspired by the industrial sounds of such bands as Mute's own Einstuerzende Neubaten, and enabled by Miller's purchase of a Synclavier synthesizer,[5] which made sampling easy, they went out and captured their own sounds. They jackhammered concrete, bounced ping-pong balls, and slammed pieces of iron and old cars with hammers. The stunning, moody "Pipeline" was composed entirely of sounds the band made themselves, with the vocals recorded in a tunnel. Its lyrics are cryptic—talking about working on a pipeline and some Robin-Hood type stuff about taking from the greedy and giving to the needy. It's a metallic hymn from some post-industrial crumbly-concrete Utopia.

I had always assumed that the cover, a photo of a muscular man swinging a hammer in a Soviet-ish fashion in front of the Matterhorn, was fake: its colors and hyperreal gloss seem too good to be true. It turns out that photographer Brian Griffin brought a model to Switzerland to have him swing a hammer in front of the actual Matterhorn.[6]

Construction Time Again moved DM into the world of ambivalent feelings and topical issues. It received a rave review in *NME*, proclaiming that Basildon's finest were socialism's new heroes[7] "Everything Counts," its biggest single and standout track, references suntans and grins and contracts and, famously, grabbing hands grabbing all they can.

"Everything Counts" is a landmark moment for DM. Gore was moved by the poverty and inequality he saw on their recent tour through Asia. In the video,[8] the rock-solid bassline is represented by real instruments, instead of the synth elements found in the recording. Wilder plays a marimba, Fletcher a shawm, and Gore, a recorder. Gahan, a human dancing tornado, is off by himself ripping up the studio floor, superimposed over shots of Berlin. He's looking smooth with a flattop hairdo with blond highlights on the tips.

The rest of the group is shown standing together, staggered in order of height, singing the chorus. They look like teens you might see in a corny video series for high school French learners: Andres, Alain et Martin.

"Everything Counts" made me furrow my brow and nod my head in recognition. Greedy corporations were already getting my goat. One of my favorite TV shows at the time was "Fight Back! With David Horowitz." Each episode, Horowitz, a reporter, and consumer advocate, explored shady companies and shoddy products. He closed each show by saying "Stay aware and informed, Fight back, and don't let anyone rip you off!"

In the *L.A. Times*, a review of *Construction Time Again* said that the "cute English techno-wimps" were originally known for creating lightweight synth-pop but with their third album, had moved on to other issues—the "sweater boys" had grown up.[9]

106.7 is No. 1

In January 1982, the *New York Times* noted that AOR, while still rockin' the United States, was taking a few hits—KROQ was ascending the charts in L.A., in tandem with WLIR and its KROQ-based format. While "Stairway to Heaven" remained the most-requested and—played song on American AOR, the times were "a-changin.'"[10]

In July 1983, *TIME* ran an article about the popularity of "New Music,"[11] featuring "post-punk" artists such as Adam Ant and Culture Club, unknown to people over thirty. MTV was a factor in its popularity, but video games were also falling out of fashion. From 1979 to early 1983, ten to twenty-four-year-olds, who made up a large part of music industry sales, were spending more money playing Space Invaders and Galaga in arcades than on records and tapes. (These interests converged briefly in March 1982 when "Pac-Man Fever" made it to No. 9 in the Billboard chart.)

However, the most powerful force for music remained radio, with KROQ leading the charge. As a testament to KROQ's influence, after KROQ jock Richard Blade put local, unknown band Berlin on the air, 25,000 copies of Berlin's *Pleasure Victim* were sold in Southern California.[12]

TIME concluded that "KROQ was now the No. 1 rock station in the large Los Angeles radio market."

Spot the Future Rock Legend

Over in Blighty, Gahan appeared on "Pop Quiz," a weekly quiz show where teams of pop stars answered questions about pop music.[13] Gahan's team was him, ELO's Bev Bevan, and Andy Mackay from Roxy Music (who published his own excellent book on electronic music). They faced Robert Plant's squad— "Sarah (sic) from Bananarama" and "Ex-Squeeze man Glenn Tilbrook."

Plant, craggy, wearing a curly mullet, roguish unbuttoned shirt, and a necklace, is an astonishing thirty-five-year-old dinosaur. It's only three years since Zeppelin broke up but he's an emissary from a different epoch. Completely affable, he's your friend's uncle who turns out to be surprisingly not creepy—just fun.

Gahan, the "kid" on his team, is chubby-cheeked, soft-spoken, and wearing a coat and tie. His big moment is naming all the members of Duran Duran for a win.

Plant's team, of course, won.

I keep wondering if Plant and Gahan spoke at all. If there was something in the air around Gahan that hinted at what was to come. Did Robert Plant know he was looking at a future rock monster? A peer in the rare world of frontmen? Would Plant have believed you if you told him?

It's five years until *101*.

Notes

1. Patrick Goldstein, "A Day of Horror at CBS Records," *Los Angeles Times,* August 22, 1982. https://www.newspapers.com/image/401030307

2. Spence, *Just Can't Get Enough*, 210.

3. Tom Taylor, "Sex, Drugs, and the Devil in the Swimming Pool: The Various Demonic Hauntings of David Bowie," *Far Out Magazine,* March 21, 2021. https://faroutmagazine.co.uk/the-haunting-of-david-bowie

4. Simon Reynolds, *Shock and Awe*. (New York: HarperCollins, 2016), 544.

5. Spence, *Just Can't Get Enough*, 209.

6. Ibid., 214.

7. Ibid., 216.

8. Depeche Mode, "Everything Counts," July 11, 1983, video. https://www.youtube.com/watch?v=1t-gK-9EIq4

9. Craig Lee, "Depeche Mode Grows Up," *Los Angeles Times,* December 4, 1983. https://www.newspapers.com/image/6 33694602/?terms=%22Depeche%20Mode%20Grows%20 Up%22%20%22Craig%20Lee%22%20&match=1

10. Robert Palmer, "In Hard Times, Pop Music Surges with Fresh Energy," *New York Times*, December 26, 1982, ProQuest Historical Newspapers: The New York Times with Index, pg. H21.

11. J.D. Reed, "Music: New Rock on a Red-Hot Roll," *Time,* July 18, 1983. https://content.time.com/time/magazine/ article/0,9171,950986,00.html

12. Ibid.

13. BBC1, "Pop Quiz," June 18, 1983, video. https://www.youtube. com/watch?v=ueGqCC-D9TY&t=4s

5

Dreamboats and Market Shares

The King of New Wave

Richard Blade was the perfect person in the perfect place at the perfect time as the Second British Invasion swept over the United States. He was English, which had all kinds of cachet, and he had a secret weapon when it came to getting new English records before anyone else: his father, back in England, who would mail records to him.[1]

Blade, formerly Richard Sheppard, originally from Torquay, England, had a unique knack for making opportunities happen. He landed in Los Angeles after becoming a successful DJ in Europe. He was successful playing parties in L.A. but his dream was to work in radio, so he set out to do that, hustling and climbing the FM ladder in places like Fresno and Bakersfield, landing at last at KROQ. (Blade, 2017)

One of the things I really like about Blade is that he always gives 110 percent. He's as enthusiastic playing "Blue Monday" on his satellite radio show as he was back in 1983. Blade was always palpably thrilled to meet musicians who came by the station or his daily after-school video show, *MV3*.

I was shocked to recently learn that *MV3* only lasted for less than a year because it made a huge, indelible mark in my brain. Blade had two co-hosts; one was a pretty girl; the other was a guy with a curly semi-mullet who was supposed to be the comic relief, I think.

The show featured local kids dancing to new-wave classics, in front of videos, in their favorite outfits, feeling so cool. There was always a kid in a porkpie hat skanking and girls with lopsided haircuts and fingerless gloves.

If I could capture some of the joy I felt listening to KROQ and watching *MV3* during this period, I would bottle it and use it to cure humanity's woes, but alas.

I remember seeing DM's "Everything Counts," "See You," and "Meaning of Love" videos on *MV3*. Not having cable TV, I could only see videos on *MV3* and a network show called "Friday Night Videos" that came on late Friday night and leaned heavily on stuff like Lionel Richie and Loverboy that you couldn't care less about.

After *MV3*, Blade hosted other shows such as *Video One* and *VideoBeat*. He achieved a new-wave gold medal when he appeared on *Square Pegs*, a beloved sitcom that aired for one season on CBS, featuring two awkward girls (Sarah Jessica Parker and Amy Linker) and their travails at Weemawee High.[2]

Square Pegs is an important new-wave text. Created by *Saturday Night Live* writer Anne Beatts, it showcased several new-wave acts: Devo played at a bar mitzvah, the Waitresses performed the title theme and appeared in an episode playing at a school dance. It also featured the most new-wave character to ever appear on television, or probably anywhere: Johnny

"Slash" Ulasewicz, played by the incandescent Merritt Butrick (who played Captain Kirk's son in the stone-cold classic film "*Star Trek II: The Wrath of Khan*"). Johnny Slash was continually clarifying his musical position: "I'm not punk, I'm new wave. Totally different head. Totally."

He was always decked out in new-wave fashion such as pink pants and vintage Hawaiian shirts, with ever-present sunglasses and a braided rat tail. Johnny and his band, Open 24 Hours (changed to Open 48 Hours), performed two songs in the series ("I'm Tired"[3] and "Get Back to Me"[4]) and they are actually pretty great.

An article in Rolling Stone from April 1983 about *Square Pegs*, said, about KROQ, that in L.A., "Every cool dial is tuned to KROQ. Especially in *Square Pegs* land. Weemawee is spiritually KROQ."[5]

Arguably the face and voice of new wave, KROQ star Richard Blade had his own little media empire in the Southland—and his favorite band was DM.

European and Sticking with It

In *Cash Box* in April 1983, Gore and Fletcher dropped some truths.

Gore said that, in the face of pressure to go back to a "dance" sound, he was going to write what he wanted to write, regardless of what was popular at the moment.

Fletcher lamented that DM had been lumped in with Duran Duran and Spandau Ballet in Europe, despite being a totally different kind of band. "If you're labeled as part of a scene, once that scene goes, you go. We don't think of synthesizer bands as a type of music," Fletcher said.[6]

DM were pretty clear all along about what they were or were not but people just didn't or wouldn't listen. What they were offering: original songs and original sounds that weren't part of any particular category, which continually stumped critics who blamed their lack of imagination on the artists themselves. "I don't get this, therefore it's not up to snuff in some fashion. Furthermore, their young audience is really enjoying it and I don't understand why and that makes me cranky. Additionally, their dance beats and lack of manly guitars make me uncomfortable because I don't dance, even at weddings."

1985 proved to be a watershed for DM in sunny SoCal. Their latest album, *Some Great Reward*, spawned a hit single, "People Are People," which went to No. 13 on the Billboard chart in August.[7]

The next year, Dennis Hunt, in the *L.A. Times*, wrote that the Palladium's 4,000 seats sold out instantly, and that California was DM's biggest U.S. market. Despite having sold only 100,000 copies of *Some Great Reward*, their audience was continuing to grow, even though Wilder said that the band wasn't going to alter their music to suit American tastes. "We're not desperate to have a hit in America. We consider our music very European and we intend to keep it that way."[8]

Hunt concludes that, unless they change their music, DM weren't going to make it in America. "Its music—all synthesizer and no drums or guitar—is just too offbeat for pop radio."

Bugs Bunny in Drag

DM were often assailed as "wimpy"; maybe they gave people the wrong idea with all that leather and lack of guitars. Gore's leather miniskirt drove critics insane; not knowing how to categorize it, they just cast him as being freaky as hell. But was he? Was it all that bizarre? Guys wearing eyeliner, lipstick, tons of hairspray, and feminine fashions weren't uncommon in the 1980s. Heck, the first time I saw a heterosexual lite-metal Poison album I thought "Ew, those ladies should really take that makeup down a notch—they look like drag queens/beauty pageant contestants."

Why did Gore confound them so?

Simon Frith, in his 1985 essay "Confessions of a Rock Critic," describes, while being a critic at large, being repeatedly asked to explain Culture Club. "I couldn't give much of an answer, just reply that the sexiest performer I'd seen was, in fact, a boy in DM, a dyed blonde in a mini-skirt and skimpy top. His shoulder straps kept slipping, leaving me, a 'heterosexual' man, breathlessly hoping throughout the show to get a glimpse of his breasts."[9]

It's the whole "Bugs Bunny in drag" thing—when Bugs gets all tarted up in lipstick and falsies and his foe, Elmer Fudd, gets big heart eyes, only to realize to his chagrin that that sexy lady rabbit was only his foe, Bugs.

The terrifying thing, somehow, is realizing that it's the getup that's sexy, and if you place any reasonably good-looking man in it? The cockles may be stirred. If Gore, with his doe eyes, beautiful skin, and lacy underthings made a man feel a little funny—Goddamnit, that lil' guy is a WIMP! A FREAK!, said the male music critic, angling to get a gander up Mart's skirt as he skedaddles stage right after the last encore.

A friend of mine once said that Gore must be "knee-deep in pussy" and it's kind of stuck in my head. It's a weird visual, but it somehow makes sense. Were the small songsmith to wander off the stage he would undoubtedly be engulfed.

Femininity is perhaps the ultimate show of masculinity, said Ben Fong-Torres in relation to Mick Jagger's flouncing and nail polish. Who's more confident than that?

Shaking the Chandeliers

In an *L.A. Times* review of DM's sold-out Southland shows in late March 1985, Terry Atkinson said that the group had outlasted other British bands popular in the early 1980s, thanks in part to its subversive sound. DM's enthusiastic fans followed Gahan's cues, raising their arms and singing into his audience-pointed mike. When Gore, sporting the magical black leather skirt, came forward to sing a song, "female screams shook the chandeliers."[10]

Undoubtedly, Gore had taken a turn at the mic to sing every girl's favorite industrial piano ballad: "Somebody."

I sometimes long to experience certain cultural moments in real-time instead of retroactively. An obvious example is wishing that I could have seen the Beatles on Ed Sullivan and lived through the Beatles' career as it unfolded. I have a younger friend who admitted that she was jealous of me for having lived through the Southern California Night Stalker killings as they happened. I assured her that it really wasn't fun at all.

There's one moment I was privileged to experience in situ. It was listening to *Some Great Reward* for the first time having no idea what was going to happen. The record's first single, "People Are People," of course, was immediately engraved on one's DNA. The industrial clangs and clinks and the video with the lads ringing bells and using wrenches and closing hatches on a warship were iconic. The shock and delight of hearing "Somebody," a piano ballad, on a DM record was one of life's rare ambushes of maximum delight.

"Somebody" was recorded in the cellar at Hansa studio with Wilder on piano and Gore[11] on vocals. Gore felt the need to get real and went *au naturel*. Wilder tactfully angled the piano away from him. "Somebody" is a little ballad about Gore's longing to find somebody and enjoy a relationship filled with mutual respect and love and healthy give-and-take, snuggling, and gentle comedy: "All the things I detest, I will almost like." Of course, Gore still doesn't want to be "tied to anyone's strings" and offers a meta-commentary on the entire exercise: slurpy ballads usually gross him out but he's going to get away with it. That sly devil. Gore has said many times that people don't get the humor in some of his lyrics. For example, in "Somebody," his imaginary girlfriend will listen when he talks about "the world we live in and life in general." The band's tour video from the *Some Great Reward* tour is called *The World We Live in and Live in Hamburg* which always makes me laugh.

Gore's performance of "Somebody" in *Live in Hamburg*[12] is about as good as this song gets. He's maximum cute: young and big-eyed, clad in a black leather jacket sans shirt, a little black leather cap, and a big floof of curly blond hair falling over his face. His voice is liquid, golden, clad in an aurora of pure feeling. It's sweeter than any DM song has any right to be. The audience is hoisting sparklers aloft which gives the whole thing an enchanting feel. I miss breaking out a lighter at appropriate moments during shows but, you know, fire safety and all that. "Somebody" is genius because it's both treacly but just knowing enough for a teen to feel sort of mature about it. I figured out how to play it on the piano (with both hands!), and felt my feelings.

"Master and Servant" was played so much on KROQ that it became like ambient noise. Sometimes you might feel inclined to change the station if your mom was driving—songs like "Sex" by Berlin (which was about singer Terri Nunn's escapades with Richard Blade)[13] or "Erotic City" surely did. But one day I found myself absentmindedly singing along with the chorus and snapped out of it for a moment—but nothing was registering on the driver's side either. In fact, my mother's fingers were lightly tapping the steering wheel.

So if you're wondering if a song that is obviously about BDSM could get played enough that no one would care or notice? The answer is yes. Thanks, KROQ, for that priceless memory. I got that it was about kinky stuff with whips and whatnot but the "kinda like capitalism" point escaped me. I thought he was just saying "What's the point of being kinky when you're simply re-enacting awful behavior?"

Some Great Reward had other gems—Wilder's last song in the DM catalog—"If You Want." I love it. It says, "Come with me if you want to liberate yourself from your humdrum existence—then qualifies it! "Even though you may not want to." One wonders why there wasn't any quality control on the lyrics but whoever let "We could build a building site" pass muster wasn't being a good friend or colleague. The middle eight of this song is absolutely bonkers and alone a standout in the DM catalog.

The album features one of my favorite Gore vocals in "It Doesn't Matter." The song's delicate plinky-plonky accompaniment is poignantly reminiscent of a broken music box or janky old ice cream truck. Gore is having a relationship that isn't going too well. He's embarrassed and overwhelmed when the other person shows him some respect—because he doesn't deserve any. It fades to a lovely outro that disappears into the air, taking my heart with it.

Bummertown, U.S.A.

Southern California is surely over-represented in the media. All over the world, images of palm trees, surfers, convertibles, chicks in bikinis, and so forth are a programming staple. It has a lot of allure: don't get me wrong. In the right light, in the right season—it's downright heavenly.

Can't say there was ever a shortage of things to do when I was a teen. A more existential boredom had set in, though.

The uncanny winds and white sky and hot, hot roads—I think DM tapped into a latent SoCal industrial vibe. Metal and concrete are as Southern Californian as Vans, sunglasses, tans, convertibles, palm trees, chaparral, serial killers, car crashes, droughts, earthquakes, rain, fast food, oranges, and so on.

It can feel a little weird to feel bad in what is purportedly the No. 1 feel-good place on the planet. I'm reminded of the eternal disappointment of people who visit Hollywood Boulevard and the Walk of Fame only to be appalled at what is actually there: sad gift shops and drifters.

Local L.A. band X had an album called *Under the Big Black Sun*. I inherited that album from one of my older brothers and thought it was pretty cool. I recall standing at an X show at a Catholic boys' school in my Esprit combat boots, wondering if I could find a date for the Christmas dance. Punk rock!

SoCal Sads

Someone I think really personifies the SoCal Sads is Dennis Wilson. The cute Beach Boy, the drummer, the youngest of the Wilson brothers and the only one who actually surfed, ran with a different crowd than Brian and Carl. He was part of a group of cads who called themselves the Golden Penetrators and were out to, uh, penetrate as many ladies as possible. He got mixed up with the Manson Family and things just went awry.

Just take one listen to Wilson's rendition of "You've Got to Hide Your Love Away" on *Beach Boys Party!* The album was meant to have the live, sing-along feel of a party, but all the partygoers were friends and family members faking party sounds in the studio.

It's a huge step up to the mic moment and Wilson nails it. The pathos in every single word he sings is palpable. Check out his "Forever" on *Sunflower*. It's gorgeous, a "rock and roll prayer" according to Brian Wilson[14] (White, 2000).

Wilson released an excellent solo album, *Pacific Ocean Blue*, got kicked out of the band for substance abuse and absenteeism, married five times, and, at the age of thirty-nine, drowned in the Pacific.[15]

Black Celebrations

You might think that it's too hot to wear black from head to toe in southern California and you'd be right. Still, that hasn't stopped generations of teens from becoming the absence of colors. Light-stealers.

Yes, I did wear black on the outside because black is how I felt on the inside as well as quite uncomfortable in that hot sun. In a cooler climate to the north, my high-school BFF, Justine Bonner, and I once got heckled by frat boys in Berkeley while accidentally walking down fraternity row while wearing black sweaters. "Nice sweaters!" called out Jeff or Brian.

That incident has stuck in my head. In the years since I pondered what was happening in the unseen brother's mind. He was met with a crossroads. Two girls were walking by and he felt like he needed to say something. Traditionally, you either state that the girls are ugly (barking like a dog, etc.)

or pretty (howling like a wolf, etc.) But he froze. He didn't know if we were ugly or pretty. He couldn't decide. The black sweaters jammed his circuits. He didn't know what we were but had already committed to saying something. So, he told us our sweaters were nice.

Something was changing and he didn't like it.

There's a long tradition of songs about people wearing and feeling black (the color!). Johnny Cash was the Man in Black. The Beatles got all Everly-Brothers sad with "Baby's in Black." The Stones, of course, wanted to Paint It, Black. I think of Laurel Canyon being all hippy-dippy and earth-toned but drunk Dark Christmas rock n' roll crooner Jim Morrison was also on the scene, wearing black leather pants and fancying himself a shaman.

Wearing black felt like freedom, I suppose. No one wore black t-shirts in the 1970s except for rock bands and metal dudes. Average teenage girls weren't dressing for funerals on any random Tuesday.

Cultural moments seem to spontaneously bloom, but there are usually clues that went unnoticed along with the way. I believe that when Bryan Ferry dyed his hair black in 1970, he set the 1980s in motion.

Notes

1. Richard Blade, *World in My Eyes*. (BladeRocker Books, 2016), Kindle, location 2981.

2. Ibid., location 3663.

3. Embassy Television, "Square Pegs," Episode 8, November 2, 1982, video, 1:20. https://www.youtube.com/watch?v=zq4JGjcQT40

4. Embassy Television, "Square Pegs," Episode 9, November 29, 1982, video, 1:02. https://www.youtube.com/watch?v=b5CNGzsU54U

5. Lynn Hirschberg, "'Square Pegs:' The Grody Bunch," *Rolling Stone,* April 14, 1983. https://www.rollingstone.com/tv-movies/tv-movie-news/square-pegs-the-grody-bunch-57888/

6. Fred Goodman, "Coast to Coast," *Cash Box,* April 9, 1983. https://archive.org/details/cashbox44unse_42/page/26/mode/2up?view=theater

7. "Hot 100," *Billboard,* August 3, 1985. https://www.billboard.com/charts/hot-100/1985-08-03/

8. Dennis Hunt, "Depeche Mode Gains Fans despite Critics," *Los Angeles Times,* March 29, 1985. https://www.newspapers.com/image/390737195/?terms=depeche%20mode&match=1

9. Simon Frith, *Music for Pleasure: Essays in the Sociology of Pop.* (Cambridge: Polity Press, 1989), 163.

10. Terry Atkinson, "Depeche Mode Steps Out beyond Mere Survival," *Los Angeles Times,* April 1, 1985. https://www.newspapers.com/image/390761194

11. Depeche Mode, "Depeche Mode: 1984 (You Can Get Away with Anything if You Give It a Good Tune)," 2006, video, 29:23. https://www.youtube.com/watch?v=OSoI6MAjQ1w

12. Depeche Mode, "The World We Live in and Live in Hamburg," December 9, 1984, video, 4:52. https://www.youtube.com/watch?v=66nmHGyvj-M

13. Blade, *World in My Eyes,* location 4288.

14. Mikael Wood, "In the '60s, the Beach Boys Were Gods. By the '70s, 'Has-Beens.' But It's Not That Simple," *Los Angeles Times*, August 27, 2021. https://www.latimes.com/entertainment-arts/music/story/2021-08-27/beach-boys-surfs-up-sunflower-feel-flows

15. Adam Webb, "The Lonely One," *The Guardian*, December 14, 2003. https://www.theguardian.com/music/2003/dec/14/popandrock

6

Uneasy Listening

Screams for Teens

I have a lot of fond memories of listening to DM while tanning, or trying to, with my high school BFF Justine Bonner. I asked her if she had any memories of listening to DM with me. "We used to listen together and we would also listen separately on our Walkmans," she said. "Mostly, what I remember," she said, "is listening to you listening to DM on your Walkman and singing along."[1]

She asked me: why did I like them so much? The first thing that popped into my mind was "They gave me permission to feel bad." Sure, there were other suburban-blues musical providers and I liked a bunch of those too—mope-rock bear-market titans such as the Smiths, the Cure (when not cute and quirky), and Tears for Fears (but only *The Hurting*). The latter inspired Justine and me to try primal scream therapy, not knowing anything about it other than Curt Smith mentioning it in interviews. We "did the work" by screaming as loud as possible for fifteen minutes or so, until a neighbor called my mom to ask if everything was OK over there.

She came to check on us, perturbed. Were we OK? We were more than OK. We were *great*. All that screaming made us feel physically exhausted but exhilarated. Jolly and refreshed. I don't know what my mom said to the neighbor but I'm pretty sure "Oh, it's fine, they were just trying some primal scream therapy" wasn't it.

There was definitely competition for the Melancholy Walkman Award but DM took it. They just *got* me.

What Kind of Celebration Was That Again?

When it came time for the boys to make their next album, obviously, another trip to Berlin was in order.

This is where I like to imagine the leather-clad DM, and fabric-clad Daniel Miller and Gareth Jones standing in a circle. Miller declares that it's time for the lads to follow their own dark star and get as grim as they like. Someone breaks out a large and extremely sharp pocket knife. They pass it around, each slicing his hand horizontally and then there's a lot of commotion and paper towels and blood and yelling for supplies.

In reality, instead of going in a more commercial, audience-pleasing direction, the band wanted to get darker and weirder. Miller encouraged them to go where they wanted to go.

Black Celebration's sleeve, another Brian Griffin production, went a bit wrong. Griffin intended for a kind of spooky, totalitarian, Naziesque structure, but it didn't quite get there. It was like when you're cooking something and it tastes wrong so you keep trying to correct it until it becomes inedible.

The cover is very "downtown prom in semi-fascist regime" which actually was kind of appropriate. Little graphics for each of the songs were embossed, glossy, black. It's a mess. It also has hideous yellow and red lettering with the band's name and record title.

When I brought *Black Celebration* home, I regarded the record with suspicion, examining the sleeve before I dropped the needle. Was this going to be DM's *Seven and the Ragged Tiger*?

It was not. It starts with a trifecta of genius. The album is called *Black Celebration*. The opening track is called "Black Celebration." The first thing you hear is a few ominous synth arpeggios and clinks and then Gahan's right there on the job, crooning: "Let's have a blaaaaack celebration." It's all a bit Spinal Tap to me. In a great way.

Then we're right into "Fly on the Windscreen." Flies on the windscreen, lambs to the slaughter—it just made sense. Life was terrifying and dark—some, if not most, of the time.

Then, one of my favorite Gore songs: "A Question of Lust." It starts out with the famed "Be My Baby" beat, buffeted by a gathering gloom cloud that tips you off: this isn't the Ronettes. (Theo Cateforis, email message to author, March 8, 2023)

It's a stone-cold classic in the "Rock and roll is coming between us, and I love you baby, but you're just going to have to accept that" category. "Beth" by Kiss is a prime example—Peter Criss's girlfriend is calling on the yellow hall phone in the hall outside the studio but he and the boys are playing. And. They. Just. Can't. Find. the. Sound. And he really would like to come home but he might be there all night.

Gore is a vulnerable, fragile baby who needs to be treated gently. The thing is? He'd never hurt his lady on purpose. And seriously? He needs to drink waaaay more than she thinks he does before he gets down to business with groupies. His tolerance is high and she's underestimating that, which kinda stings, honestly.

In the end, he's off on another tour, but you know, he'd rather be home instead of tripping balls and boning chicks but he's going to do that anyway. This song is staggering—Gore's vocals on the chorus are so plaintive you really do want to pat his fluffy head and tell him it's OK. You're not going to let what you built up crumble to dust over lust and trust issues. You love him just the way he is.

"Stripped" is monumental. Beginning with a sample of Gahan's Porsche, it's atmospheric, lush. I always imagine myself lying on the forest floor with a leather jacket under my head to keep the pine needles out of my hair, in a big urban park that contains some kind of liminal space where you can get lost.

"You're breathing the fumes/I taste when we kiss." That's it.

Not "But Not Tonight"

Black Celebration was dark and gloomy but DM's moment, it seemed, was ripening.

Sire seized that moment by not putting out "Stripped," but rather, instead, "But Not Tonight," which was from a soundtrack from a movie called *Modern Girls*. The weird thing is that I've seen many, many, low-quality 1980s movies, but I had never seen this one until recently.[2]

So, I watched it. It's a perfect example of the 1980s "wacky" aesthetic. Three "girls" or young women in their 1920s share an apartment in L.A., have meager/nonexistent incomes, and have one zany night having "hilarious" adventures. It's like Martin Scorsese's *After Hours*, a movie that Justine and I loved, but not very good.

There's one thing that's true in it. One of the girls calls a hotline that tells you where the "underground" clubs are happening. That existed. My friends and I used to call it and then go to illegal warehouse parties downtown until all hours, typically bringing our own tequila or whatever we could get our mitts on and washing it down with juice boxes or sampling the $3 all-you-can-drink grain alcohol punch. They were simpler times.

"But Not Tonight" flopped.

It's the opposite of "Black Celebration," which invites you to … have a black celebration and celebrate another awful day gone by. "But Not Tonight" talks of getting away from "pointless debauchery" and feeling the rain on one's face and more alive than one had in years. It makes me uncomfortable.

Not a Depeche Mood at all.

Our Band of Choice

Naturally, on the way to the *Black Celebration* concert at Irvine Meadows, where we were driven by the older cousin of one of my friends, the car kept breaking down and we had to pull over so she could pop the hood and pour water in there somewhere.

The Irvine Meadows show felt like a big sing-a-long with around 16,000 of your friends, or people that you would probably hate if you went to the same school with, but would defend vociferously if it came to it. Just cozy as hell. We giggled quite a bit about how dorky Gahan was with his skinny white arms, and hilarious calls and responses—just yelling incomprehensible syllables into the mic and holding it out to the audience who weren't quite sure what to do.

In a review of the concert, Chris Willman in the *L.A. Times* wrote that DM had somewhat stealthily become the band of choice for young Angelenos, being far more popular in the Southland than elsewhere in the United States, baffling parents concerned about their darkness and rock fans who objected to their lack of guitars.[3] He suggested that people freaking out about heavy metal's buffoonery might want to consider why 16,000 youngsters were enthusiastically singing along with "Blasphemous Rumours," with its gimlet-eyed view of God. He touches on Gahan's pelvic thrusts and rawk exhortations, and Gore's bondage getup, then concludes that "When you're selling out the Forum, even a black celebration can be a happy affair."[1]

Michael Lev, in the *San Pedro News-Pilot*,[4] noted DM were one of the most popular bands in Southern California, while the rest of the country lagged behind. He found it refreshing that there was no long hair or guitar solos at the show—despite the fact that Wilder, Gore, and Fletcher reminded him of "Nazi Andy Warhols" behind their synths and that, with all their pre- recorded material, the lads could have gone to a bar

[1]Ibid.

until the show was over. Nonetheless, he concluded, "Backing tapes, video monitors and all, this was a far more inspirational show than what usually goes on at Forum concerts, in which the languid guitar meanderings sound about as spontaneous as a home computer program of pie recipes."[5]

In the *New York Times*, reviewing shows about a month earlier, critic Stephen Holden, said that the lads had toughened up their image and music, singling out Gore, whose "mixture of satanic spikiness and pouty glamour resembles that of the pop star Billy Idol."[6]

Holden concluded, "The audience responded physically to music that has retained the regular beat of disco but with a retarded momentum and a futuristically murky ambiance."[7] I believe that is called "dancing."

Over at KROQ, things were changing. The station was sold to Infinity Broadcasting for $45 million, which at the time, was the highest price ever paid for a radio station.[8] About the sale, former KROQ DJ Swedish Egil said, "It had to happen. It became a big, popular station, someone else was going to come in and take over the station, take control of it."[9] (Ohanesian, 2007)

More changes were on the way.

Notes

1. Justine Bonner, interview by Mary Valle, May 14, 2021.

2. *Modern Girls,* directed by Jerry Kramer. (1986; Los Angeles: Amazon, 2012). https://www.amazon.com/Modern-Girls-Cynthia-Gibb/dp/B007HCI588

3. Chris Willman, "Depeche Mode's Dark Message," *Los Angeles Times,* July 15, 1986. https://www.newspapers. com/image/402377537/?terms=depeche%20mode%20 mode%27s%20dark%20message&match=1

4. Michael Lev, "Despite Lack of Airplay, Depeche Mode a Sell-Out," *San Pedro News Pilot,* July 11, 1986. https://www. newspapers.com/image/607513927

5. Ibid.

6. Stephen Holden, "Music/Noted in Brief; The Clangorous Pop of Depeche Mode," *New York Times,* June 11, 1986. https:// nytimes.com/1986/06/11/arts/music-noted-in-brief-the- clangorous-pop-of-depeche-mode.html

7. Ibid.

8. *Broadcasting,* "1986 Was the Year of the Sale; New Records Set for Stations and Cable Systems," February 9, 1987. link.gale.com/apps/doc/A4676963/ ITOF?u=baltctycpl&,sid=bookmark-ITOF&xid=d2d42f12

9. Elizabeth Ohanesian, "Modern ROQ: The Oral Histories of Dormer KROQ DJS Dusty Street and 'Swedish' Egil Aalvik." (Master's thesis, California State University Northridge, 2007). https://scholarworks.calstate.edu/concern/theses/ jm214t80q?locale=pt-BR

7

America, Man

Welcome to Reagan Country

I was out trick-or-treating on October 31, 1980, when one of our neighbors dropped a bag of red jelly beans—branded with the Republican elephant logo in my pillowcase, with a conspiratorial twinkle. The dad in question chortled something about voting that clown out of office. I felt the breath of evil on the back of my neck.

Regardless of the fact that my parents were Republicans and pretty much everyone they hung out with were, too, and that I had indeed supported President Ford in the '76 election (chanting Ford! And! Dole! In front of the TV, where I spent a lot of time), I had parted ways with the G.O.P.

California, as a popular bumper sticker said, was Reagan country. Reagan had held court as the Golden State's governor from 1967–75. An avowed hater or universities and free speech, he advocated a "bloodbath" was a great way to deal with protesters in Berkeley. A few days later, four unarmed student protestors were killed by the National Guard at Kent State., a tragedy that spurred two witnesses to form new-wave giants Devo, whose work explored the alienation of living in a society where truth no longer mattered.[1] In 1980, the aw-shucks authoritarian became the U.S. President, promising to make America great again.

The United States was having another one of its identity crises. The 1970s sputtered out in a blizzard of coke and bad vibes, with dirty little suburban urchins roaming the streets, fifty-two American hostages being held prisoner in Iran, and progressive younger folk clashing with their elders, as in *All in the Family,* a dreary issues-oriented sitcom that ran from 1971–9.

The main character, Archie Bunker, is a working-class white bigot who regularly clashes with his sideburned, liberal son-in-law about hot topics including rights for women, Black people, and gay people; abortion, and Vietnam; wanting nothing more than for society to revert to the good ol' days when people just didn't talk about that stuff. Sounds familiar.

The solution was to elect an elderly faux-cowboy with weird, dyed, Brylcreemed hair and rouged cheeks. Reagan promised to bring us back to cornfields, and baseball, and apple pie, and white men doing whatever the fuck they wanted, whenever the fuck they wanted to, which is actually the entire reason for America in the first place so yeah: we were getting back to basics.

Nuclear Tears and Fears

People might think the 1980s in the United States for angsty young white teens were all about hairspray, clove cigarettes, and Sprechgesang, but we had some existential crises as well. The United States and the Soviet Union were locked in a cold war that involved a lot of bloviating about nukes.

In an era of only a few TV stations, television events still meant something. One of those events was *The Day After,* a TV movie about America getting nuked. Everyone had to watch it and feel a little uneasy the next day. The movie didn't really live up to the hype—but it was an ABC TV movie so what could you expect, really?

I had already decided that my nuclear war strategy would be to run in the direction of the blast, hoping that I would get immediately zapped. Who would want to live as an irradiated ghost, coughing up blood, just waiting for the poisoning to finish the job? Not me. I'd rather be dead, I said at the time. Still, the thought of getting nuked did trouble me at times. I really hated being in the clutches of two assholes who just wanted attention.

There were a lot of pop songs about nuclear war, some of which I've been singing for decades but had no idea about. "99 Luftballons?" Thought it was about the feeling of childhood passing. "I Melt With You?" I thought it was about doing it but it turns out that "melting" was being nuked.

Frankie Goes to Hollywood's "Two Tribes" summed up the situation succinctly, stating that, in so many words, there are no winners when it comes to war. The video featured sumo wrestlers representing the cold-warring "superpowers." I maintain that warring leaders should be forced to play ping-pong, compete in potato sack races, or just go at it mano a mano and leave the rest of us out of it. I had no problem with Russia! They loved their children too, didn't they, Sting?

In the 1983 film *War Games*, a movie about a teenage boy who almost causes a global thermonuclear war, a computer concludes:

"The only winning move is not to play."

It was a pervasive feeling of cognitive dissonance—sure, things were supposed to be all hunky-dory in the 1980s? It was all facade. Music was there for the young people who just didn't buy it, whatever it was.

Gettin' Real in the Land of the Free

British bands have a long history of getting all down-home and "Murican, based on fantasy notions of 'rootsy' chilling sessions in an imaginary Mississippi delta somewhere settin" on a porch with elderly Black musicians who think they are really really good for white people to being all cool and New Yorky and "street" and everything in between. I call this mood "America, man." The Rolling Stones walked both of these paths, from the Gram-Parsons-inflected country-style "Dead Flowers," to funk-rockish "Shattered," where Mick Jagger yells about things you might find in Manhattan: pride, joy, love, sex, work, success, rats, crime, bedbugs, and so forth.

The Beatles sometimes donned cowboy hats and chewed on pieces of straw—Paul and his "Tucson, Arizona" and Ringo's first country outing—"Act Naturally."

Zeppelin, of course, spent quite a bit of time in the imaginary Delta of Blues with, among others, "When the

Levee Breaks" and also had their minds blown by the West Coast scene in "Going to California."

Inspired by their travels throughout the United States, Duran Duran paid tribute to the former colonies on their 1982 magnum opus, *Rio*. "My Own Way" finds Simon Le Bon yelling "I'm on 45 between 6th and Broadway" which was "a rough approximation of the address for the popular New York club *The Peppermint Lounge*: on 45th street between 6th Avenue and the Broadway theatre district," according to Annie Zaleski in *Duran Duran's Rio*.[2]

They also rhymed "Rio Grande" with "sand."

Billy Idol's whole "punk Elvis" act is pure "I dig America." He drank an entire bottle of cough syrup (for laughs) and freaked out on a 48-hour bus trip from Canada to New Jersey, giving us his immortal "I'm on a bus, on a psychedelic trip, reading murder books and trying to stay hip" lyric from "Eyes Without a Face."

In "Hot in the City" he yelled "New York!" in a climactic burst. He also yelled "Amarillo," "Boston," "Minneapolis," "New Haven," "Chattanooga," cand "Sioux Falls," depending on the market.

English new-wave pop star Kim Wilde updated the world on what was happening with America's youth in "Kids in America" in '81. She let everyone know that from "New York to East California, there's a new wave coming, I warn ya." In Kim's POV, that new wave stopped at Needles.

David Bowie has a whole "America, man" section in the record bin of his career but he was so self-aware I don't count it.

U2 didn't hide their fascination with the Home of the Brave. They had songs called "MLK," "4th of July," and "Elvis Presley and America" on their 1984 release *The Unforgettable Fire*. Things got a little personally dystopian for me when U2 issued copies of 1987's *The Joshua Tree* to every single person I knew, and we had to listen to it whether we liked it or not. Bono got super thoughtful about, if I remember correctly, JFK's assassination, persecuted immigrants, and Jesus roaming the Home of the Brave. For the cover, Anton Corbijn immortalized the band in black and white in Death Valley, trying to look all tough but deep.

I once took a field trip to a visible section of San Andreas Fault in a school van, with the headmaster at the wheel. We listened to *The Joshua Tree* all the way there and all the way back. In a singular act of devotion, in the hottest part of summer 1987, a host of rock critics crawled through the Mojave Desert on their hands and knees for forty days and forty nights just to show how much *The Joshua Tree* meant to them. Thirty-seven survived.

The Joshua Tree now resides in the Library of Congress's National Recording Registry. In an accompanying essay, Stephen Cantanzarite says, of the album, "It's become ingrained in the popular imagination—particularly in America, the country whose myths, legends, and ideals inspired its creation."[3]

Well played, U2. Well played.

DM had resisted "America, man" for quite some time, but when 1987 rolled around, they too, took the bait, setting the stage for what was to come. They recorded a cover of Bobby Troup's 1946 classic, "(Get Your Kicks on) Route 66," which had been covered by a ton of other people including Bing Crosby, the Rolling Stones, Billy Bragg, and Joe Strummer's pre-Clash band, the 101ers.

"Route 66," although a B-side, got plenty of play on KROQ. In fact, it was No. 1 on 1988's top 106.7 list. It made an ideal song to use in the *101* documentary as well.

One month before "A Concert for the Masses," J. D. Considine, writing for the Baltimore Sun, called the Ritz-Carlton in Chicago to speak with Gore.[4]

In the finest rock 'n roll tradition, Gore was checked in under an alias. Considine had to ask for "Mr. Presley."

In the *101* documentary, Gore and Fletcher are seen shopping at a music store in Nashville. Gore picks up some tapes, including Johnny Cash, who will later cover his "Personal Jesus," which was inspired by Priscilla Presley's *Elvis & Me.*

The "kids on the bus," fans who were filmed during their journey from Long Island to Pasadena, on the other hand, are grossed out/bored by a stop at Graceland.

Of course, the whole vintage Caddy, leather jacket, football stadium theater of DM's "A Concert for the Masses" announcement is nothing but America, man.

A New Depeche Mood

"A Concert for the Masses" was the culmination of the band's *Music for the Masses* tour. After the heavy, claustrophobic, Teutonic darkness of *Black Celebration,* the band left Berlin behind and hired Dave Bascombe, who had produced Tears for Fears' massively popular *Songs from the Big Chair.*

Music for the Masses was meant to be ironic given DM's reputation as the band of choice for black-clad depressives, but it turned out to be prophetic. The record begins with the iconic single "Never Let Me Down Again," a behemoth that opens with a drum sampled from Led Zeppelin's "When the Levee Breaks" and a heavily processed sample of a Gore guitar riff. It's a new Depeche Mood.

"Never Let Me Down Again" was seemingly built for a stadium. It signals a new direction for the band, with its hard-hitting sound and sense of motion. *Music for the Masses* is the sound of a band hitting its stride. Containing *101* highlights "Strangelove," "Sacred," and "Behind the Wheel," *Music for the Masses* was a chart-topper in spirit. It has perhaps been obscured by the bright light of *101*.

The album's cover, an image of totalitarian-ish megaphones on a post in front of sunset over a buildingless, unpopulated expanse of desert-like terrain. It's a bit underwhelming.

This is DM's last album cover not created by Anton Corbijn.

The band met Corbijn, a Dutch photographer, when he was dispatched by the *NME* to shoot the lads for a cover story during the *Speak & Spell* era. Clarke didn't show and Corbijn slyly turned the band portrait inside out—Gahan, although front and center, is completely out of focus, leaving Fletcher and Gore in the spotlight.

In the *Music for the Masses* era, Corbijn directed black-and-white videos for "Never Let Me Down Again" and "Behind the Wheel." With Corbijn's input, DM began to change its image. He went on to serve as the band's creative director for decades.

Corbijn did the seemingly impossible: he made DM look cool. He also added a missing element to DM's hodgepodge of videos: women. i.e., "Yeah, these dudes get laid, too. By ladies."

It was only a few years ago that I realized "Never Let Me Down Again" was quite possibly about drugs. I took it at face value—just a guy and his best buddy hanging out, driving around in a car. Specifically, guys like Gore and Fletcher. Fletcher spent a lot of time riding with his best mate, Gore, to places all over the world. Flying high, watching the world pass them by,[5] etc. Gore has always kept his lyrics vague to leave room for interpretation, so there is no right answer. But I think it's about him and Fletch.

In November 1987, *Cash Box* reviewed "Never Let Me Down Again:" "Yet more dark, brooding pop from the boys of Depeche Mode. Band is steadily establishing themselves in the States and could cross over the Top 40 market soon."[6]

Author Andrew Goodwin, in *Dancing in the Distraction Factory: Music Television and Popular Culture*, said that the visuals in the "Never Let Me Down Again" video let the world know that "the band (and its fans) are 'serious.'"

Perhaps America's 80's bluster was waning. In *Circus of Ambition: The Culture of Wealth and Power in the Eighties*, author John Taylor (not Duran Duran's bass god) said that groups such as the Smiths, the Cure, and DM expressed a general malaise: "Life to them was bleak, morose and miserable." He goes on to suggest that, similarly to the late 1960s, "Bull market bands with songs about love and fun were giving way to bear market bands that dwelt on violence and alienation." On October 19, 1987, known as "Black Monday," the Dow Jones Industrial Average lost 22.6 percent of its value, at the time the largest single-day stock market decline in its history.

Notes

1. Tim Sommer, "How the Kent State Massacre Helped Give Birth to Punk Rock," *Washington Post,* May 3, 2018. https://www.washingtonpost.com/outlook/how-the-kent-state-massacre-changed-music/2018/05/03/b45ca462-4cb6-11e8-b725-92c89fe3ca4c_story.html

2. Annie Zaleski, *Duran Duran's Rio.* (New York: Bloomsbury Academic, 2021), 38.

3. Stephen Cantanzarite, "The Joshua Tree—U2 1987," *Library of Congress National Registry,* 2013. https://www.loc.gov/static/programs/national-recording-preservation-board/documents/U2JoshuaTree.pdf

4. J.D. Considine, "Depeche Mode: Rooted in Rock," *Baltimore Sun,* May 27, 1988. www.newspapers.com/image/377877002

5. Andrew Goodwin, *Dancing in the Distraction Factory: Music Television and Popular Culture.* (London: Routledge, 1993), 88.

6. "Feature Picks," *Cash Box,* November 14, 1987.

8

KROQ's Woodstock

Music for the Masses

According to Richard Blade, in early 1988, Sire Records's Howie Klein and Seymour Stein cooked up an idea: a stadium concert, with a KROQ band. Klein met with Richard Blade three weeks before the leather jackets-convertible-Rose Bowl announcement. "A Concert for the Masses" was set in motion.[1]

The last rock concert at the Rose Bowl was the AOR poster-child Journey on July 2, 1982. Journey, supported by Blue Öyster Cult, whose signature hit, "Don't Fear the Reaper," provided a fresh twist on the ol' "might as well do it because we're going to die anyway" theme, and Canadian rock champs Triumph and Aldo Nova. I imagine the atmosphere of that show being like that described by Paul McCartney in "Venus and Mars/Rock Show:" sports arena, colored lights, scoring some coke, long hair, referring to a guitar as an "ax," etc.

The Journey lineup curiously foreshadowed A Concert for the Masses—Journey and DM became Eternal Giants; BÖC (like OMD) are still rotated in and out on the classic rock/classic alternative station; Thomas Dolby and Wire, like Triumph and Aldo Nova, still have their own special followings.

"A Concert for the Masses," along with announcing that "alternative" music was, well, not so alternative anymore, marked an important occasion for KROQ—its tenth anniversary. Ten years earlier, when KROQ gave birth to the 80s, the nation seemed caught in an eddy of unknowing, which is where we found ourselves in 1988. Reagan's reign ended, and the presidential race was tepid at best: Vice President George H. W. Bush versus Massachusetts governor Michael Dukakis, who was most memorable for an awkward photo op riding in a tank.

DM were at a turning point in their career—so too was KROQ, which had begun billing itself as the "Rock of the 80s and 90s," which felt odd: their brand was "Rock of the 80s." What was happening? Known things were slipping away on all fronts. Meanwhile, the station had become more dependent on "classic" KROQ tunes.[2]

In a year-end roundup of significant music events, *Cash Box* observed that DM, "a band that's built its oeuvre out of gay bondage imagery," packed the Rose Bowl with "80,000 L.A. suburbanites."[3]

I hadn't really given any thought to going to the Rose Bowl show. However, the day before the concert, I heard that KROQ was giving away tickets in exchange for canned goods for a food pantry. "Why not?" I thought, and got the tickets.

The day of the show KROQ jocks were broadcasting live from the Rose Bowl, giving a lot of traffic updates to people driving in from every direction. Justine and I, along with a few of our high school classmates, arrived during OMD's set and parked ourselves way up in the stands at the far edge of the bowl. I don't mind bad concert seats—sometimes being too close to performers can feel a little too personal. I also don't like any situation where I might be crushed or trampled to death. I do, however, like having multiple exit points and the ability to scurry out at any point.

It's a good thing we didn't have awesome seats anyway. We didn't know this at our high altitude but people were going berserk down in front and having a massive food fight. I would not have liked that.

It was so bad that Richard Blade had to tell everyone to take a chill pill.[4]

Then Came the Rain

Perhaps it was the company, perhaps it was Gore's God-bothering, but the Concert for the Masses, in part, felt like a special Mass at Dodger Stadium with Pope John Paul II, which had occurred the year before. I think I went to it, but I don't know for sure. That churchy feeling was confirmed when the band launched into "Blasphemous Rumours." About the song, Gore said that he went to church for a few years, but wasn't ever devout. "And I was more of an observer you know, every week, like a prayer or when everyone would be praying for them. And inevitably, like everyone died on the prayer list. It seems to be like the worst thing ever to get on the prayer list."[5] Of course, I was sitting with a gaggle of girls from my Catholic high school. "Blasphemous Rumours" has always struck me as hilarious, campy like "Seasons in the Sun" and "Alone Again, Naturally," which is not a bad thing. I love all three.

I wasn't the only person who felt that way: Gore said that one possible name for *101* was "Mass."

Freedom Rock and Magic

As night fell, I felt a tap on my shoulder to find a friendly old hippie couple seated behind us. The lady handed me a pipe. I passed it down to my friends, then partook again on the way back. Then "Triumph of the Will"-style banners fell to the haunting strains of "Pimpf," an instrumental from *Music for the Masses*. Naturally, "Pimpf" was the name of the Hitler Youth magazine.

I laughed, thinking about the commercial for *Freedom Rock*, a compilation album of 1960s songs.[6] In the commercial, two old hippies are hanging out in lawn chairs near the back of their van. When the opening riff of "Layla" comes on, one says "Hey man, is that Freedom Rock?" *"Yeah, man." "Well, turn it up, man!" Freedom Rock* was four records, three cassettes, or four CDs full of hits by the original artists—such as Ramblin' Man by the Allman Brothers, "Somebody to Love" by Jefferson Airplane, and, inevitably, "Free Bird" by Lynyrd Skynyrd. To this day, there are certain riffs that make me want to tell someone to turn that Freedom Rock up.

Our new friends were Freedom Rockers, for sure, and that was hilarious, but there was something else going on. I had an uncanny feeling. Have you ever felt time slide in front of you, leaving you with a glimpse of the past and future—simultaneously? Maybe it was the weed but the moment waterfalled right in front of me. The hippie couple were trying to tell me something. And that something was this: I was watching my own Freedom Rock unfold in real time. This event was already falling into the past and almost felt like it had already happened.

I felt a chill. DM were a rocket heading to the future and Wire, OMD and Thomas Dolby were being cast off—boosters falling into the void. I was shucking off high school, DM, and my friends and heading into the darkness of space as well (or college).

All the people around me—except for the hippie godparents—didn't realize it but it was crystal clear. The 80s were dying in real time.

DM came on like the chosen ones. Gahan reached an apogee that night. Gone were the blazers and leather pants that he had worn on stage before. He had ascended to the Freddie Mercury outfit, which seemed as inevitable as standstill traffic on the 405. He started out with a leather jacket, which was shed rather quickly, revealing a white button-up shirt and white jeans. The button-up shirt was tossed into the audience and Gahan reigned, resplendent in a white tank and jeans.

After watching a Led Zeppelin concert, William S. Burroughs wrote, "The essential ingredient for any successful rock group is energy—the ability to give out energy, to receive energy from the audience and to give it back to the audience. A rock concert is in fact a rite involving the evocation and transmutation of energy."[7]

Saying that magic is the origin of all arts, the rock star: a priest, magician—dare I say healer?—leads the ritual, during which performers and audience create communal energy—magic. This is where Gahan found himself—in the realm of the gods, surrounded by a black-clad heavenly host.

When he spontaneously waved his arms to and fro during like windshield wipers during "Never Let Me Down Again," he was greeted with the sight of 120,000 arms doing likewise, a field of pale, squiggly wheat.

As the singer in a synth band, he was alone but yet, was backed up by his own legion. Wilder, the good musician, Andy, ever supportive, and a shadow wizard: Gore. The power and electricity of being the conductor is undoubtedly powerful. But consider Gore. Quiet, somewhat inscrutable, the man who creates what DM is at its core: its songs.

So, while it would be astonishing to lead the ritual, imagine that you're Gore, playing your keyboard, occasionally singing a song, observing it all. Imagine an entire stadium full of people singing your songs, that you pulled out of the ether. That's the sun behind the sun.

Banger after Banger

The band, in fine form after 100 shows, brought it. *101* is a good primer (i.e., Depeche Mode 101) and a testament to the quality of Gore's songwriting, Gahan's powerful voice, Wilder's sound design and, while Fletcher didn't really play all that much and his microphone was never plugged in, he's there too. As Antoine de Saint-Exupéry wrote in *The Little*

Prince, quoted in a million high school yearbooks, "It is only with the heart that one can see rightly; what is essential is invisible to the eye." Sometimes it might even be unheard by the ear.[8]

101 is banger after banger. Different arrangements, live instruments (not all of them, obviously), three-part vocal harmonies, and the enthusiasm of the crowd make it hum with energy.

An unexpected highlight is "Pleasure, Little Treasure." It was a B-side that was B-side material. But live, it was a rock 'n roll rave-up, complete with some rad guitar work by Gore. It's raucous fun, and in the *101* documentary, Gahan breaks out maximum ass shakes and a nifty move where he pelvic-thrusts across the stage, holding his mike at crotch level. The crowd goes nuts. The only thing it's missing is a classic band-intro during "Pleasure, Little Treasure's" jam break. I wish he'd bellowed, "On keyboards! The sultan of sound! Alan Wilder everyone! Near a keyboard! Everybody give it up for Andy Fletcher, the dancin' machine! And right here we've got Mr.! Martin! Gore!"

The concert's closing song, "Everything Counts," turned into a spontaneous extended audience singalong, after the tapes stopped. Wilder kept playing the melody while the audience repeated, "Their grabbing hands/grab all they can/ everything counts in large amounts."

Which was weirdly self-reflexive. Indeed, we were a large amount of people—approximately 60,000—singing about everything counting in large amounts, while the band made a large amount of money. Corbijn's *101* cover design is a DM merch table featuring a poster with Corbijn's classy black-and-white portraits of the band.

Gahan began weeping after the show. He immediately felt that it wasn't ever going to get any better than that.

Daniel Miller, backstage, beamed with pride. His Silicon Teens had become Silicon Men.

Richard Blade felt a unique sense of oneness with the universe. The Boys from Basildon were going to conquer the world.

The Night the 80s Died

I didn't think about the Concert for the Masses for thirty-three years. But while perusing the internet in the middle of the night, I happened upon a reference to a Dave Gahan side project. "Dave Gahan," I thought. "Huh."

Then I gorged on everything DM. I saw photos of generations of fans posed in front of the Rose Bowl. Apparently, the Rose Bowl show was kind of a big deal? I had no idea.

Justine and I had not spoken of it, either. I asked her what she remembered. I recalled that the concert felt slightly uncool. Justine said it was indeed uncool and the venue was also uncool. "Super uncool," I said. DM were suddenly a little bit embarrassing. We had just graduated from high school. We were chucking our adolescent enthusiasms.

"Maybe it would have been more fun if we had been sitting next to each other," she said, since our other friends were between us. "Maybe," I said. "Could have actually been worse if we both felt a little weird. But at least the Freedom Rockers were there." "That helped," she said.

Yet, we danced and sang along with every song. Just said she said she was worried about finding the car at the end of the concert. "I felt clammy," I said. "It was a reality where I no longer belonged. Although maybe that was the weed?" No, that wasn't it. Without it, I would have felt a little panicky about making our way through enthusiastic fans walking slowly, savoring the moment.

"It was the night the 80s died," I said. She said, "I felt it, too."

Things always seem the same, until they don't.

Notes

1. Blade, *World in My Eyes*, location 7706.

2. Patrick Goldstein, "KROQ Klassics: Riding an Old Wave," *Los Angeles Times*, September 21, 1986. https://www.newspapers.com/image/402414586

3. Joe Williams, "Music '88: Alternative Rock," *Cash Box*, December 31, 1988. https://archive.org/details/cashbox52unse_24/page/n1/mode/2up

4. Blade, *World in My Eyes*, location 5515.

5. Martin Gore, interview by Denis McNamara for WLIR, June 7, 1986. https://dmlive.wiki/wiki/1986-06-07_WLIR_92.7,_Garden_City,_NY,_USA

6. "Freedom Rock Commercial," January 14, 2008, video, 2.0. https://www.youtube.com/watch?v=2eGWW8KOQio

7. William Burroughs, "Rock Magic: Jimmy Page, Led Zeppelin, and a Search for the Elusive Stairway to Heaven," *Crawdaddy*, June, 1975. https://arthurmag.com/2007/12/05/willima-burroughs-onled-zeppelin/

8. A. De Saint Exupéry, *The Little Prince*. (San Diego, New York and London: Harcourt Brace Jovanovich, 1971), 87.

9

No DM, No Nirvana: *101* and Its Legacy

The Road to Rawk

The *101* album and same-named documentary came out in March 1989. The *101* documentary was directed by the late D. A. Pennebaker, who made, among many others, *Don't Look Back* and *Ziggy Stardust and the Spiders from Mars*. Pennebaker and Chris Hegedus, his wife and filmmaking partner, had a whale of a time making it. In a summary of the film on their website, they say, "We always tell people that the time we spent on the road with Depeche Mode was our favorite film adventure."[1]

The documentary has some great concert footage. It captures DM's unique blend of textured, moody, synth-based music, with Gahan's bigger-than-life frontman act, pelvic action, butt wiggling, and lots of rock exclamations. He's out there giving infinity percent.

I must say that at the DM concerts I attended, it never occurred to me that the band wasn't playing all the music live. Who cares? I think they have a perfect live blend that hits the ear just right. Different enough to be compelling, and no gross jam sessions or song mutilations.

There are also some comedic bits, such as when Gahan is trying to figure out how to greet the crowd. Wilder says, "Why not say, good evening, welcome to 'A Concert for the Masses?'". To which Gahan replies, "Who do you think I am, fucking Wordsworth?"

101-the-movie shows Fletcher breaking the band down in an interview. "Martin's the songwriter, Alan's the good musician, Dave's the vocalist, and I bum around." Ah, Fletch. You were too modest. Fletcher did administrative tasks, served as a group spokesman and liaison, was a good sounding board in the studio, and helped with intra-band communications. At their shows, he danced and clapped with zeal, serving as a sort of surrogate for the audience. Somehow, Fletcher was in DM and also DM's No. 1 fan. He was also Gore's best friend.

In a review of the *101* album and film, Jon Savage said in the *Observer*, that DM were "mildly miffed that it is under-appreciated in Britain, due to an emphasis on 'authenticity' expressed in the country's interest in roots and 'new country' music."[2]

Fletcher said that America doesn't have a problem with that. "They had been fed authentic music for so long in the States," he said, "that they want something different."[3]

DM felt the need to get super "authentic" themselves after 1990's *Violator*, widely considered to be their masterpiece.

In 1993, DM released *Songs of Faith and Devotion*.

Does this album feature guitars, drums, backup gospel singers, and a church organ? You bet it does. The video for

"I Feel You," the record's first single, presents a different sort of DM. Gahan has gone all long-haired and grunge; Gore is rockin' out on a guitar, and Wilder is unrecognizable behind a drum kit, throwing his bobbed hair around, wearing sunglasses. Who even is this band?

DM rocked out in all the other ways that count during this era. Gahan, lamenting the world's lack of real rock stars, took it upon himself to rectify that situation: moving to L.A., growing out his hair, and becoming a heroin addict. Gore descended into alcoholism. Fletcher had to leave the tour because of a mental health crisis. Wilder, who had repeatedly mentioned in interviews that he didn't want to be a pop star in his forties, had some workplace issues. After giving his all, shaping the band's sound, working overtime in the studio, and so forth, for years, he felt underappreciated and unacknowledged. Eat a peach, in other words. One day, he issued a scathing memo and squealed out in his Mercedes, flaming tracks in the metaphorical company parking lot.

Thus closed DM's "imperial era," coinciding with the rise of 1990s "alternative" rock. Grunge was all about being "authentic" to the point of not showering, wearing tattered garments, and having nothing but pure, 100 percent guitars and live drums. Other than being completely "authentic" there was some Depecheness that carried over. Men with baritones ruled the day and a certain sensitive, petite blond fellow who liked to wear dresses enchanted teens with his feelings.

Those of us who enjoyed the androgyny, color, innovation, and unmanliness of 1980s music had to come back down to earth. Perhaps we had flown too close to the sun to think that men with guitars weren't going to come back. Not counting men with guitars like, you know, R.E.M. or the Plimsouls or the Replacements.

However, like punk before it, grunge turned out to be ....rock. Just rock. Mainstream grunge was the AOR of the 1990s and the classic rock of the not-too-distant future.

It's Not "Live," It's Live

In 1989, Jon Pareles in the *New York Times* wrote an article complaining about lip-syncing the live performances, leading with a description of a recent Bananarama show, and laments that the Bangles, "a solid enough rock band with a No. 1 hit," used canned drumbeats for some songs on their current tour. He then criticizes DM for releasing a "live" double album, although the members only add keyboard lines and vocals to taped backup. The album, he said, "promises to be invaluable for collectors of crowd noise and between-song patter."[4] Which is … most live albums?

He lamented the existence of lip-sync competitions throughout the nation's schools and even—on television.

He said that live performances offer a chance to see what can be done with "naked hands and throat and hips and feet." OK, I think DM covered that. And stuff about "doing something difficult and rare, demonstrating skills beyond those of most of the audience." Check. He accuses "lip-syncers and canned bands" of "taking dictation from machines … giving up autonomy to avoid risk."

If playing the Rose Bowl, having a rockumentary made by prestige filmmakers, and yes—a spontaneous singalong—

isn't authentic, I don't know what is. DM sound great in concert. They sound great on a live album. With different arrangements, live instrumentation (yes), and the unflappable energy of Gahan out in front (with Andy Fletcher cheering in the back), they are an incredible live band. It's hard to believe, but four men with three synthesizers and a tape machine rocked the hell out of 60,000 people in Pasadena, California, on June 18, 1988. If we didn't have evidence, you might not believe that it's true, but luckily, we do.

Why DM, though?

Dusty Street said that you never really know how things are going to happen for bands in terms of success. "You go and create your art and hope that people like it, obviously." But there are factors that can help: "It also depends on the record label you've got behind you and Depeche Mode were lucky to have Daniel Miller, and he was an absolutely brilliant man. He knew exactly how to promote Depeche Mode."[5]

The Birth of Modern Rock

Billboard kicked off its "Modern Rock" chart in late 1988. "Alternative" music was here to stay. By headlining the Rose Bowl as a relatively unpopular band on a national level, DM kicked the doors open for the mainstreaming of "alternative" music, tilling the soil for Nirvana's breakthrough.

That same year, the *L.A. Times* reported that KROQ, having fallen to No. 16 in the ratings after an eighteen-month slump, was changing its tune. Dusty Street was out—Guns 'n Roses, Faith No More, Tom Petty and the Rolling Stones were in. New station manager Trip Reeb said, "We're going to be a rock station." He explained, helpfully, "A station playing harder-edge, guitar-oriented music."[6] Hell yeah!

In general, the late 1980s were a no-person's-land of musical dregs. Annoying songs by once-cool 1980s artists filled the airwaves—1988's top 106.7 top 10 includes "Peekaboo" by Siouxsie and the Banshees, along with cheesy novelty hits by "Harley David (Son of a Bitch)" by Bullock Brothers and "Wild Thing" by Tone Loc, for all you lovers of getting drunk in Tijuana. 1989 brought us "Stand" by R.E.M. and "Love Shack" by the B-52's, a perfect selection for when you want to do karaoke and you hate yourself.

The Red Hot Chili Peppers, having hung around long enough, finally got their chance at the big time.

"The music just started to kind of suck," said April Whitney.[7]

Dusty Street said that KROQ's evolution was bound to happen. "Music changes all the time. Every ten years it will change fairly drastically. It will always change. It's inevitable because younger bands are coming up and they're talking about what they're talking about. And they're expressing what's going on in their life."[8]

I asked her if she thought there was anything about Southern California in particular that made DM so popular there.

"Well, no, because I think younger people were receptive to it because there was a huge swath of the country that was also joining us at the same time. WLIR in Long Island was not playing exactly the same stuff. They weren't playing

Oingo Boingo, but they were playing more Television and New York Dolls. Every major market had its own punk/new-wave thing happening.

"Every generation has their own music. And if you're playing the music of that generation, you're going to have the listeners from that generation. KROQ simply stepped into a vacant lot and said, 'Hey, here's your music.' And we were the only ones in town."[9]

KROQ had moved to Burbank. The new station was roomy, the equipment always worked, and there were vending machines. Richard Blade, said, "But for everything we gained, we lost the thing that was most vital to KROQ and had distinguished us from everyone else in radio, our freedom."[10]

Jocks would no longer be able to choose a song not on the playlist and share it with listeners. There would be no more informality. The new building was guarded. Friends and listeners could no longer drop by.

The jocks' choices shaped the station's music. It was non-market-research based. According to Swedish Egil, sometimes Carroll would tell him to pick up the list on his way to work, then he'd say that he would bring it in the morning, but no playlist would be there. In those days, the jocks could "go berserk and play anything we wanted."[11]

The idiosyncratic nature of KROQ's playlist, which came from Carroll's gut feelings, the jocks' choices, and the amount of calls for requests a song would receive, was literally handmade at first. What made KROQ great was jettisoned completely for a completely predetermined playlist. Street had been used to playing several picks per shift and she wouldn't comply with the new management.

April Whitney said, "I had kind of a family feeling—I'd been there a long time and you know, kind of felt like there was some sort of sense of family, but then the corporation came in and really took that away." She misses the irreverent sense of humor that the jocks brought to KROQ. It was, after all, a station that played "Teenage Enema Nurses in Bondage" by a group called Killer Pussy. "It was okay to make fun of anything. It was OK to make fun of ourselves."[12]

Rick Carroll had been going back and forth from the station through the 1980s but returned in 1988. Sadly, he died the next year from HIV.

It is estimated that, today, six corporations own 90 percent of all media in the United States, KROQ among them.

"A Concert for the Masses" was more than a tenth-anniversary celebration for KROQ; it was a requiem Mass. KROQ, as we knew it, was gone.

Freedom Rock, the Sequel

I asked another high school friend, Colleen Rice Nelson, who spent a goodly amount of time at KROQ hanging out in the booth, meeting bands, even dropping off muffins on the way to school, what made KROQ so compelling.[13] She said, "The KROQ DJs were real people, playing real bands in a real place—in Pasadena, and the DJs weren't too much older than the listeners."

Colleen was, of course, right down in front of "A Concert for the Masses," but she was so close to the stage she could hardly see. Maybe being a seat-filler in the bleachers wasn't so bad after all?

"It wasn't 100 percent Depeche Mode fans there, anyway," she said. "People came because it was a KROQ concert. It was part of our identity. It was the only place in Southern California you could hear a lot of those bands."

It seemed so corny at the time, but my radio was always tuned to 106.7. It was a constant, and the jocks' presence was comforting.

I imagine Justine and I in some of our 80s regalia doing a commercial in some mythical analog era for our own *Freedom Rock*: a fifteen-record set called *Roq of the 80s* which would have songs from the original artists including: Slow Children, Dramarama, Toy Dolls, Cee Farrow, Black Flag, Belouis Some, Gene Loves Jezebel, Sugarcubes, XTC, Untouchables, Fun Boy Three, Romeo Void, Big Country, Time Zone, Joe Jackson, Icicle Works, the Stranglers, The The, ABC, Scritti Politti, Japan, Grandmaster Flash and the Famous Five, Real Life, Teardrop Explodes, Icehouse, Strawberry Switchblade, the Glove, the Damned, Alphaville, Blancmange, Style Council, Dead Milkmen, Dead Kennedys, Fad Gadget, Wide Boy Awake, the Fixx, Burning Sensations, Q-Feel, Toto Coelo, Aztec Camera, Squeeze, Tones on Tail, Love and Rockets, Lords of the New Church, Red Rockers, B-Movie, Propaganda, Alphaville, Freur, JoBoxers, Polecats, Pete Shelley, Peter Schilling, Payolas, Divinyls, Howard Devoto, the Alarm, the Nails, Jim Carroll, Wire Train, Lene

Lovich, the Bongos, Trans-X, Fishbone, the Untouchables, the Belle Stars, Plastic Bertrand, Barbie and the Kens, Haysi Fantaysee, Bow Wow Wow, the Vandals, Felony, Plimsouls, Tonio K, T.S.O.L., Stacey Q, They Might Be Giants, Suburban Lawns, Three O'Clock, Animotion, Agent Orange, Ultravox, Ian Dury, White Horse, China Crisis, Trio, EBN-OZN, Captain Sensible, and many, many more!

I could go on.

The truth is, even though I was a DM fan, KROQ was why I went to "A Concert for the Masses" because they gave me tickets, but also in a broader sense. KROQ brought DM into my life and then played them so much I couldn't take it anymore and you know what? I appreciate that. I didn't catch Wire or Thomas Dolby and only a little bit of OMD. I may have liked them a few years previously, but now they drove me insane, which seemed appropriate given the true nature of the occasion: a cosmic sendoff.

KROQ wore grooves in my soul, really. A few years later, when I heard the opening strains of "Come as You Are," from a college roommate who was from Seattle. This is before they were famous. He had a photo of Nirvana on his door in the "Bleach" era. I said, "Wait, is that Killing Joke?"

America's Stadium

It was a beautiful day in Pasadena when my daughter and I took a tour of the Rose Bowl. Death was sort of everywhere. It was the day after Andy Fletcher unexpectedly died. It was the day after my dad was buried on a breezy hill at Holy

Cross Cemetery, joining his parents, my mom's parents, and one of my brothers. I didn't cry at my dad's funeral. At the burial, though, since my dad was a vet, Army guys came and did the flag-draping ceremony and played "Taps." And that is when I bawled.

The Sierra Madre mountains loomed majestically all around us. The Rose Bowl is tucked into the Arroyo Seco, or Dry Gulch, which contains a river that flows from the San Gabriel Mountains to the Los Angeles River, then out to the Pacific. If it is flowing, that is.

Walking through the tunnel into the stands to the location of the stage, I thrust my arms in the air and said, "Good evening, Pasadena!," imitating Gahan's voice-cracked greeting in *101*. I could detect an imperceptible *something* of that night still hanging in the air, decades later.

The Rose Bowl is halfway underground—it was made to have a low profile so as not to obscure its glorious location. The tunnels, that is, are at ground level. The "bowl" was dug out by men with mules and shovels just about 100 years ago.

The view from the field is a little different. I looked up at the bleachers where I stood with my high school friends. They were very far away.

One of my fellow tourists, a sports fan, knelt down reverently on one knee and touched the sod, the bowl's own proprietary blend, according to our guide. I bent down too and gave it a poke. It was springy, high-quality.

Later, we were told that this will probably be the last grass field at the Rose Bowl for the time being due to upcoming water restrictions. Residents would only be allowed to water their lawns once a week from there on out. "It's never coming back," said our tour guide, who was a hearty, relaxed, retired guy, a Stanford grad with a big gold Rolex enjoying his afternoons. Law or real estate, I wondered. It was a toss-up.

"Pretty soon, California's going to have to go to war over water rights with Colorado and Arizona," he said, chuckling in a "Glad I'm not going to be around for that" way.

The Rose Bowl is an even odder setting for DM's first American stadium show than I remembered. It's beautiful, quaint, well-designed, lost in time, somewhat magical.

The tour guide mentioned concerts at the Rose Bowl but the only references to DM I find are in two places—one in the Rose Bowl museum in the concerts section (U2, who came later, feature far more prominently) and another in the locker room, which has a timeline running around the top.

I was snapping a few photos of the DM timeline panel when a guy asked if I went to the show. I said yes and he confessed that he loved DM and they were all over his playlists. He would have loved to see them live, however, he didn't think his wife would want to go. She pretended not to hear him. He shrugged in my direction, hoping for help from a third party. I wasn't getting involved. I looked away.

Reaching Out, Touching Faith

While I wrote this book, I listened to *101* a lot, especially when I drove to and from my monthly maintenance treatment for metastatic breast cancer, which I'd been living with for about five years at that point. I always went alone to these appointments; it was easier that way. I don't like to admit weakness or ask for help, which might be a problem, but on the other hand, this attitude has gotten me through some stuff.

The record was bracing. Listening to the massive sound of Gahan, Gore, Fletcher, Wilder, and the tapes, of songs I could recognize if you merely tapped out the rhythm on my arm, I was overcome with emotion, and that emotion was gratitude for everything I've been able to experience during my life. I thought about all the concerts I've seen and the friends who joined me. I thought about the outrageous good luck of getting free tickets to go to a concert when I was feeling over it. While feeling cranky. While feeling, actually, sad. I was losing a lot at the time and ambivalent about what was coming next.

How delightful and wondrous it all was. Decades later, I am able to write about it. I have met with insanely great fortune. I thought about the cheap synthesizers that existed in 1980, enabling DM to play. I thought about Daniel Miller, who gave them the support so they could soar, and Seymour Stein, who recently died, for signing them in America, for KROQ, a crazy little radio station that "smelled like pee" (according to Colleen) that brought us all together, especially its DM superfan and new-wave overlord, Richard Blade, along with the rest of the jocks, including the inimitable Dusty Street and insightful April Whitney.

I listened to the "Everything Counts" singalong and thought, Justine and I are on this record, too, in that crowd, singing, no matter how uncool we thought it was. We're there together for all eternity, or at least as long as DM records exist.

So, although I didn't feel the magic at the time—*101* played the long game.

Naturally, Justine and I saw DM at Madison Square Garden during their tour supporting *Memento Mori*, their first post-Fletch album. The album was already in progress when Fletcher died, and Gahan and Gore decided to keep going—it's what Fletch would have wanted,[14] said Gore.

We prepared by listening to the concert's playlist beforehand. I thought it was pretty good, but it wasn't quite soaking in. My expectations were neutral before the concert. Sometimes, "legacy" concerts can feel like seeing a tribute band, which isn't a bad thing.

Special occasions call for special garb, of course. I was wearing a resplendent high-necked black "Goth Prairie" gown that swished delightfully. Justine killed it in a suit with a lemon print and a chartreuse blouse. "Guess we could have just gone with a concert T and jorts," I said, eyeing our fellow concertgoers when we arrived. "Next time," said Justine.

During a gorgeous rendition of "Enjoy the Silence," I turned to Justine and said, "THIS IS FUCKING AWESOME!" We, and the rest of the crowd were on our feet the entire time dancing and singing with gusto.

Afterward, Justine observed that the show was very much a concert of a "current" band— not one that is playing the hits and throwing in some new songs that no one really cares about. DM were a living thing, and in breathtaking form.

Those songs I wasn't sure about? Total. Bangers. Indeed, the concert inspired me to check out DM's vast post-Violator output.

Gahan and Gore played with long-established touring musicians. The drum-machine band now had a drummer with a kit that's comically, Spinal-Tap-ishly large.

Gahan was wiry and in fine voice, energetic, elegant: a dapper gentleman of rock. Gore remained cherubic in his early sixties. The stage set design (by Anton Corbijn, naturally) featured a twenty-seven-foot-tall letter M in the back that served as a screen for films. When Gore stepped up to the mic for his solo section, the M seemed like it was backing him up, personally.

"It's like his own Broadway show," said Justine. "Martin with an exclamation mark!" I replied.

Corbijn's portraits of Andy Fletcher appeared during "World in My Eyes," his favorite DM tune.

I'd say we both have some stuff going on in our lives, as do most adults, but Depeche Mode don't offer pure escapism. Their music has always embraced life's darker aspects, acknowledging that human existence can be confusing, disappointing, and downright bleak at times, which is ultimately life-affirming.

When I was a teenager, I felt seen and understood when I listened to their music. I learned that life can be difficult, but you can still dance. A "black celebration" is not a contradiction. Death is everywhere, yes, but Justine and I are still here. Still friends, still singing along and laughing.

DM are here too, and in breathtaking form. Those songs I wasn't sure about? Total. Bangers.

The show closed with "Personal Jesus," a bluesy barn-burner that was inspired by Gore's reading of Priscilla Presley's *Elvis and Me*.

With our hands in the air, we yelled, "Reach out and touch faith!"

Notes

1. C. Hegedus and D.A. Pennebaker, "Depeche Mode 101: Summary." https://phfilms.com/films/depeche-mode-101/

2. Jon Savage, "Modernists à la Mode," *The Observer,* March 12, 1989. https://www.newspapers.com/image/258997129

3. Ibid.

4. Jon Pareles, "Just Give Me a Chip Off the Old Bach," *New York Times,* January 10, 1988. https://www.nytimes.com/1988/01/10/arts/pop-view-just-give-me-a-chip-off-the-old-bach.html

5. Street, interview.

6. Patrick Goldstein, "KROQ Caught between Rock and a Hard Place," *Los Angeles Times,* October 22, 1989. https://www.newspapers.com/image/405730368

7. Whitney, interview.

8. Street, interview.

9. Ibid.

10. Blade, *World in My Eyes*, location 5716.

11. Ohanesian, *Modern ROQ: The Oral Histories of Former KROQ DJS Dusty Street and "Swedish" Egil Aalvik*, 85.

12. Whitney, interview.

13. Colleen Rice Nelson, interview by Mary Valle, November 19, 2021.

14. Dave Heching, "Depeche Mode Releases First Song since Death of Founding Member Andy Fletcher," *CNN,* February 9, 2023. https://www.cnn.com/2023/02/09/entertainment/depeche-mode-new-song-andy-fletcher/index.html

Acknowledgments

Thank you to Leah Babb-Rosenfeld, Boice-Terrel Allen, Dan Bukszpan, Justine Bonner, Colleen Rice Nelson, April Whitney, Theo Cateforis, Annie Ducmanis Adams, Sarah Diehl, everyone in I Listened to KROQ in the Early 80s, Enoch Pratt Free Library, Baltimore County Public Library, Timmy, FC, Gus, and all love to the late, amazing Dusty Street, who was so generous with her time. She not only made me laugh; she inspired me to rethink my foregone conclusions.

Also Available